Lexico-Logical Form

Linguistic Inquiry Monographs
Samuel Jay Keyser, general editor

Lexico-Logical Form

A Radically Minimalist Theory

Michael Brody

The MIT Press
Cambridge, Massachusetts
London, England

This book was set in Times Roman by Asco Trade Typesetting Ltd., Hong Kong and was printed and bound in the United States of America.

Library of Congress Cataloging-in-Publication Data

Brody, Michael, 1954–
  Lexico-logical form : a radically minimalist theory / Michael Brody.
    p.   cm.—(Linguistic inquiry monographs ; 27)
  Includes bibliographical references (p.) and index.
  ISBN 0-262-02390-3.—ISBN 0-262-52203-9 (pbk.)
    1. Grammar, Comparative and general—Syntax. 2. Generative
grammar. I. Title. II. Series.
P291.B75   1995
415—dc20   95-8254
                                                          CIP

Contents

Series Foreword

We are pleased to present this monograph as the twenty-seventh in the series *Linguistic Inquiry Monographs*. These monographs will present new and original research beyond the scope of the article, and we hope they will benefit our field by bringing to it perspectives that will stimulate further research and insight.

Originally published in limited edition, the *Linguistic Inquiry Monograph* series is now available on the much wider scale. This change is due to the great interest engendered by the series and the needs of a growing readership. The editors wish to thank the readers for their support and welcome suggestions about future directions the series might take.

Samuel Jay Keyser
for the Editorial Board

Acknowledgments

I would like to express my indebtedness to the following people for comments, correspondence, conversations, and other help in connection with this monograph: Gabor Brody, Annabel Cormack, Noam Chomsky, Liliane Haegeman, Hans van de Koot, Shalom Lappin, Rita Manzini, Martin Prinzhorn, Neil Smith, Michal Starke, Marcus Szigeti, Deirdre Wilson, Martina Wiltschko, and the two reviewers.

Introduction

It is a truism that grammar relates sound and meaning. Theories that account for this relationship with reasonable success postulate representational levels corresponding to sound and meaning and assume that the relationship is mediated through complex representations that are composed of smaller units. One of the most immediate questions arising from this organization of the grammar concerns the way these units combine to form a representation.

As usual in Principles and Parameters theory, let us think of sound/meaning representations as corresponding to the interface levels of the grammar, Logical Form (LF) and Phonetic Form (PF), the representation of a sentence S on these levels being **lf** and **pf**. The inventory of the units from which syntactic structures are built up is the lexicon, its output for S a set **l** of formatives. Our question is then the nature of the relationship between the set **l** and the **lf** of S.

In much work within the Principles and Parameters framework, the relation between **l** and **lf** was taken to be mediated by representations at two additional levels: D-structure and S-structure. D-structure was generally taken to be a kind of grammar-internal interface level with the lexicon. LF representations were then taken to be derived from D-structure ones, essentially through the operation of the rule of Move α. S-structure was the level at which phonological rules branch off this derivation.

Let us call a level of representation mediating between the lexicon and LF, like D-structure and S-structure, an M-structure. Correspondingly, a structure of S that mediates between **l** and **lf** is an **m**-structure of S. Note that a sentence can have more **m**-structures than the number of M-structures in the grammar: it will have an **m**-structure for each M-structure, but it may also have intermediate **m**-structures that correspond to no level of representation.

The standard view of the relation between l and lf of S was that l composes into a representation at an M-structure (i.e., at D-structure) and the representation at this level is mapped through a series of **m**-structures (including one at another level of representation, S-structure) to **lf**. This means that the grammar relating LF to PF contains two derivations. One is the phonological derivation relating S-structure to PF, the other the syntactic one relating D-structure to LF.

There have been proposals that D-structure should be thought of as an abstraction of S-structure (e.g., Rizzi 1986a; Sportiche 1983; Koster 1987). I have suggested (Brody 1985, 1987) that the basic level of representation is LF in the sense that D-structure should be abstracted from this level. This approach can eliminate all M-structures, in fact all **m**-structures. There will be no **m**-structures if the abstraction of D-structure from LF involves no derivational steps. D-structure is then to be thought of as a proper subpart of LF (cf. Brody 1991b, 1993, and chapter 1 below.) It follows also that LF is the only syntactic level if only those levels are syntactic that mediate between the lexicon and LF. In another sense, however, S-structure was taken to be a syntactic level in this LF-based theory. The LF-to-PF mapping contained a syntactic part (up to S-structure), which essentially expressed movement/chain relations, and a phonological part (from S-structure to PF).

Chomsky (1993) put forward the "minimalist" hypothesis that the grammar contains no non-interface levels. All conditions on representations hold at LF and PF, the only two levels of representation. This hypothesis, if true, strengthens the claim that LF is the basic syntactic level: in fact it is the only syntactic level at which representational conditions hold. The LF-to-PF mapping can then be purely phonological. In other respects, the assumption that D-structure is properly included in LF is stronger than the standard minimalist hypothesis. the latter claims that there are no M-structures, but from the former it follows that there are no **m**-structures either, that is no derivations linking l and lf.

In this work I shall discuss aspects of this radically minimalist approach in which the lexical input is not related to the interface level through a derivation. In this theory, semantic interpretation rules and the lexicon have access to the same interface, the level of Lexico-Logical Form (LLF).

Since languages differ, it cannot be the case that both (L)LF and the mapping from (L)LF to PF are universal. One or both of these must be parametrized. I assume that the choice between the three alternatives that arise here is an empirical matter, rather than a question of taste or stipulation. The standard view is that LF is universal, and the LF-PF mapping is parametrized. The universality of LF is often defended as a necessary assumption, based on the argument that the form of LF is not directly accessible to the language learner. All that follows, however, from such considerations is that (L)LF representations can vary from language to language only to the extent to which the language learner can determine the relevant parameters on the basis of PF data. In the absence of reliable theories of this matter it seems reasonable to assume that determining (L)LF parameters from PF is not an impossible or particularly difficult task in general. After all, (L)LF representations are regularly recovered quite fully on the basis of PF evidence.

Consider parametrization of movement/chain relations. Under theories where S-structure was taken to be an intermediate level between LF and PF (whether or not S-structure is also intermediate between D-structure and LF), this level provided a natural locus for these parameters. The standard minimalist approach is not radically different. Although the relevant parameters must now be at the interface level of PF, it is still the LF-PF mapping that will vary in the relevant respect from language to language. Under the stronger version of the LF-based approach explored in this monograph, there is no parametrization of the LLF-PF mapping with respect to the relations that are expressed in this theory in terms of chains at the syntactic interface level. The evidence presented in this work points to a conclusion with potentially far-reaching consequences, that the syntactic interface itself must be parametrized in the relevant respects.

Chapter 1 provides several arguments against syntactic derivations. I argue that chains and Move α cover the same type of relations, and that therefore one of the two concepts is redundant, and a theory incorporating both is wrong. I provide evidence for the concept of chains, and thus against movement derivations. I discuss various aspects of the LLF theory and compare it with the standard minimalist framework.

In chapter 2 I turn to the question of Subjacency. Subjacency has been claimed to be a condition on derivations and it is often assumed that overt and LF movement differ in that only the former is subject to this condition. I argue against both claims and for the position that Subjacency is a condition on all LLF chains. I adopt the position that chains that appear not to obey Subjacency are in effect parasitic on other wh-chains, and their locality properties are those of parasitic gaps.

Chapter 3 analyzes thematic properties of parasitic gap structures and reconsiders the concept of chain in this context. Some of the consequences of the parallel between parasitic gap structures and multiple wh-structures are also discussed here.

Constraints that influence the application of Move α in theories that assume this rule determine the overt position of the moved element. "Timing principles" like Procrastinate and Earliness play a crucial role in determining whether movement applies overtly or covertly. Chapter 4 provides an alternative to such derivational conditions. The principle of Transparency proposed there requires elements that correspond to the moved category of the derivational framework to be in the highest position of their chain that is licensed by morphology.

If there is no Move α, then lexical categories must occupy their PF positions at (L)LF. This generalization allows the straightforward expression by chains of the overt movement relations of the standard Principles and Parameters theory. Two kinds of relations, however, appear to counterexemplify this generalization: those standardly expressed by reconstruction and by LF movement. LF movement places a category higher than its PF position. The relations it captures are treated here in terms of expletive-associate LLF chains (chapters 1, 2, and 4).

Reconstruction effects, on the other hand, appear to show that sometimes a category may be in a lower position than where it overtly appears. In chapter 5, I adopt the copying/layered trace approach, but I argue that at LLF all copies must be present simultaneously. If this approach is correct, then no derivational mechanism (movement or deletion) is necessary to treat reconstruction, either.

I wrote the first drafts of chapters 1–4 in 1991. Chomsky's minimalist program (1993) provided the impetus to major changes in chapters 1 and 4 and the addition of chapter 5 in 1992. Some further revisions were made at various times during 1993 and part of 1994.

Chapter 1

Chains and Move α

1.1 Introduction

Assuming that chains and Move α express the same type of relation, a theory that contains both concepts is redundant. I argue in this chapter that the concept of chains is independently motivated by the principle of Full Interpretation and by the condition that determines the distribution of the set of thematic positions (section 1.2). Hence I claim that a theory that postulates movement transformations is redundant and therefore wrong. In 1.3 I discuss an explanation of the chain internal distribution of thematic positions in terms of a Projection Principle, which provides another argument against movement rules. In 1.4 I argue that a theory where the lexicon interacts directly with the interpretive-conceptual systems is superior because it does not create an infinite number of intermediate structures that correspond to no well-formed interface representation. Thus I propose that no derivation should be interposed between the lexicon and LF. I refer to this approach as the Lexico-Logical Form (LLF) theory.

In 1.5 I compare the LLF approach to the standard minimalist theory, according to which conditions on representations hold only at the interface levels of the grammar. The LLF theory will be seen to be radically minimalist: in LLF syntax there are only interface conditions since there is no syntactic derivation, and therefore there can be no intermediate structures created by the individual steps in such a derivation on which to state non-interface conditions or to which another interface level could connect. In 1.6 the explanation for the distribution of thematic positions given in 1.3 is shown to be compatible with the minimalist approach, and the organization of the LLF grammar such that SPELL-OUT can apply only to LF is argued to be superior to a theory where

SPELLOUT can apply to various points in the derivation. In 1.7 I discuss in a preliminary way the question of how the LLF theory expresses "LF movement." I propose that the positions corresponding to the landing sites of LF movement contain expletive-type elements that form LLF chains with the category standardly taken to move covertly.

1.2 Transformations and Full Interpretation

Consider a simple derivation in standard Principles and Parameters theory, like (1) and the associated derived representation in (1b):

(1) a. np was seen John
    b. John was seen t

The operation of Move α applies here to the object NP *John* and places it into the position of the subject. In the resulting structure (1b), *John* and the trace left by the operation of Move α create the chain [John,t]. Clearly the concepts of chain and of Move α are related. But they are not identical. Crucially, the concept of Move α entails that if Move α applied to an element that element will have occurred in two distinct positions in the derivation. The notion of chain involves no such assumption.

As is well known, the syntactic associations expressed by chains and Move α form a natural class, since they share a number of properties. They are constrained by dedicated locality principles like Subjacency and the ECP and have distinctive Case and thematic characteristics. These associations involve only one thematic position, the most embedded one of those in the chain, and their A-chain subparts contain only one (structurally) Case-marked position (the highest occupied A-position). Reconstruction effects (binding theoretic, thematic-idiomatic and scopal) are also generally associated with chains/Move α.

In Chomsky (1981), chains were defined independently of Move α and the operation of Move α was taken to be free, not directly constrained by chain-construction. Chains were defined essentially as an ordered set where every member binds the next and every member except the first is a nonpronominal empty category. On the assumption that Move α is also constrained by c-command, its operation always resulted in a structure that satisfied this definition: Move α always caused a chain to be formed. On the assumption that Move α was completely free of conditions, its application still corresponded to a chain in all grammatical cases in which this rule applied. This system was less than optimal: it was an accident that Move α always (or at least in all grammatical sentences) created a chain and that chains were generally created by Move α.

In fact the correspondence between chains and Move α seems even stricter. The claim that not only all movement creates a chain but also all chains are created by Move α seems to be true in all the basic cases. Consider the examples in (2), which might seem problematic for this claim.

(2) a. There arrived a man
    b. It seems that Mary is bright
    c. Pictures of himself are easy to tell John to take
    d. the headway which we made . . .

In (2a) and (2b), *there* and *a man* and *it* and the postverbal CP, respectively, arguably form chains (show the usual clustering of properties), but apparently without movement. However, given the hypothesis of LF movement and the assumption that LF and not S-structure is the level relevant for chain formation, the problem disappears. Thus, according to this approach, the associate (*a man* in (2a), CP in (2b)) moves to the expletive at LF, either replacing the expletive (Chomsky 1986a) or adjoining to it (Chomsky 1991).

(Incidentally, this is not the only way to maintain the claim that all chains are created by Move α. Another possibility is to restrict the notion of chain to associations formed by overt movement. The association between *there* and *a man* in (2a) can be taken to fall under the more inclusive concept of CHAIN. The relevant cluster of thematic, locality, and other properties can then be taken to hold not just for chains but more generally for CHAINs. The important point to note in the present connection is that both the theory that uses CHAINs and the one that makes use of expletive replacement create full one-to-one correspondence between chains and Move α, making the independent definition of these two concepts untenable.)

In (2c) and (2d), we find reconstruction effects between positions that are not standardly analyzed as being related by Move α. Thus the matrix subject and the embedded object position in the *easy to please* construction or the head of the relative and thematic position of the relative pronoun are not usually taken to be related by movement, but the examples show (anaphoric and idiomatic) reconstruction involving these positions. Similar examples can be constructed with other related structures, for example with clefts. Given such data, one might adopt a theory in which the positions involved in reconstruction can be members of the same chain even when no movement connection is established. However, I have argued (Brody 1990a, 1993) that the analysis of head-raising (i.e., XP head) should be extended to the *easy to please* type adjectival complement construction, and probably also to the other cases that can exhibit reconstruction effects. Thus the generalization that all chains are created by Move α is once again maintained. (Note that the logic of the situation here is similar to the previous LF-movement case. If, contrary to the present claim, these constructions could not be derived by movement, then we could attribute reconstruction effects to the appropriately extended notion of CHAIN and still maintain the strict correspondence between chains and Move α.)

There are two ways of expressing the assumption, now generally held, that the concept of chains and that of Move α are so strongly interrelated. Chains could be defined in terms of Move α, or it could be assumed that Move α is characterized in terms of chains. In Brody 1985, 1987 I took the latter view: I argued that the chain is the basic concept and proposed that this concept enters into the characterization of Move α: Move α is an algorithm that is restricted to operate chain internally. Chomsky (1986a) proposed the opposite approach: he postulated that chains are a "reflection of a 'history of movement.'" There appears to be no controversy in these works or elsewhere in the literature over the claim that there is such a strong relationship between the two concepts. But such a close connection, amounting to equivalence modulo the difference between derivation and representation, should raise the question: are both concepts in fact necessary?

In other words, given that chains and Move α cover the same class of phenomena, we have an argument from conceptual economy against a theory that makes use of both concepts. If Move α is independently motivated, then the theory that uses chains to capture antecedent-trace type relationships is wrong; if a principle like Form Chain is independently necessary, then a theory incorporating Move α must be mistaken.

Rizzi (1986a), noting this redundancy in the theory that postulates both chains and movement transformations, argued for assuming the existence of chains on the basis of examples where some coindexed element intervenes between two members of a chain, as for example in (3):

(3) Gianni *si*   è stato affidato t
    'Gianni to-himself was entrusted'

In (3) the reflexive clitic *si* intervenes between the passive subject *Gianni* and its trace. Rizzi argues that given the local binding condition in the definition of chains (each chain-member must locally bind the next), no chain can be formed in (3) that includes the NP *Gianni* and its trace but excludes the reflexive clitic *si*. The chain [Gianni,si,t], however, receives two theta roles and thus violates the Theta Criterion. Rizzi took this to be an argument for defining chains independently of Move α: "if chains were 'memories' associated to NPs, faithfully recording applications of 'move α,' nothing would prevent formation of well-formed chains for the ungrammatical examples ... and the proposed explanation would be lost" (Rizzi 1986a, 78).

There are certain empirical problems with the local binding condition (see, e.g., Lasnik 1985). Assume for present purposes that it is tenable. Rizzi's argument also needs some updating if, as was argued in Brody 1993, the syntactic Theta Criterion does not exist—a position adopted independently in Chomsky 1992. Although the assumption that chains rather than categories receive theta roles might well be correct, semantically there appears to be no motivation for the uniqueness requirement used here (and many other places in the literature). Chains cannot be prohibited from receiving more than one theta role on general semantic grounds, since there are cases where such assignment gives grammatical results. More than one theta role can apparently be assigned to a chain, so long as all theta roles are assigned in the same position (see Chomsky 1986a). Rather than by applying a uniqueness condition on theta-role assignment, the chain [Gianni,si,t] could be excluded using the assumption that no theta role can be assigned to a chain-member in a non-root position (see below), or that an A-chain can only contain one argument (Brody 1993) of which it is the abstract representation (Chomsky 1986a).

No updating, however, can solve the basic problem of the argument. Assuming that something like the local binding condition is responsible for the cases Rizzi discussed, it still remains to determine whether this condition should be stated on chains or on Move α. The derivational equivalent of the local binding condition is a crossover condition in the sense of Postal (1971), a condition that prohibits Move α from moving a category across a co-indexed element. Thus we have no argument for

chains here until it is shown that the derivational crossover characterization is inferior to the representational, local-binding approach. This is
in fact a particular case of a more general problem. Although a theory
that incorporates both Move α and chains seems clearly redundant, it is
difficult to decide between these two options since most conditions are
easily stateable both representationally and derivationally.

In spite of this difficulty, I shall again take up the issue of deciding
between a representational and derivational approach to Principles and
Parameters syntax (see also Brody 1985; Koster 1978, 1987; Rizzi 1986a;
Sportiche 1983). I shall argue against what one might call mixed
theories, theories that are representational at least insofar as they make
the standard assumption that the grammar contains a designated interpretive interface level (i.e., LF), but that also postulate derivational
processes. (See, e.g., Lebeaux 1989 for a version of Principles and
Parameters theory that explicitly rejects the single interpretive interface
level hypothesis. I assume that a theory with such a level is preferable
to one with global interpretation, on grounds of restrictiveness.) I shall
argue that the assumption that such an interface level exists is incompatible with a derivational approach to the chain–Move α cluster
of properties. After one such argument having to do with Chomsky's
(1986a, 1991) principle of Full Interpretation, I shall give further arguments for the same point based on the major constraint on the distribution of thematic positions.

According to the principle of Full Interpretation (FI), LF can contain
only elements that are legitimate at that level (the same holds for PF).
The legitimacy of these elements derives from their ability to receive an
appropriate interpretation provided by the grammar-external systems
that connect with the grammar at the relevant interface. Thus FI requires that no element without an interpretation appears at an interface
level.

Consider, then, traces that are not interpretable as variables, like
traces in NP- or head- or adjunct-movement/chains:

(4) a. John was seen t
    b. Jean embrasse t Marie
    c. Why did you say Mary fixed this t

Given the standard set of assumptions about the interpretation an LF
structure is to receive, it seems very difficult to provide such elements with
any interpretation at all. However, given the assumption that LF is the

sole semantic interface level, these traces have to be present here, since they are necessary to ensure correct interpretation. The NP-trace must be present to relate the argument *John* to the theta role it is to receive, the head trace to relate the verb *embrasser* to the position where it assigns its theta roles, and the adjunct trace to make it possible to relate the adjunct to the element it modifies. Thus FI appears to be violated: these traces must be present at LF but receive no interpretation. The contradiction can be resolved by assuming that chains and not categories are the elements that receive an interpretation at LF. Thus these empty categories are only subconstituents of the elements whose LF legitimacy is ensured by the fact that they have semantic content.

Suppose, then, that the notion of chains is necessary at LF, that chains and perhaps only chains are legitimate LF objects (Chomsky 1991). But if this is the case, then a theory that makes reference also to the concept of Move α is redundant and therefore wrong: the class of relations it characterizes must be characterized by the LF concept of chains for independent reasons having to do with FI.

Notice that we could not avoid this conclusion by simply reformulating FI so that it only requires elements to *contribute* in some way to the interpretation, unless we specify in what ways an element can make such a contribution. Otherwise such a reformulation would make FI vague enough to be empty. On the other hand, the proposal that chains are the elements that receive an interpretation can be thought of as specifying limits on such contribution by categories that have no interpretation themselves. The consequence of FI stated on chains is that an uninterpreted category can be present and thus contribute to the interpretation when it is part of a chain that also contains an interpreted element.

The argument has the same logic as the argument for the rejection of a syntactic LF Theta Criterion in Brody 1990a and 1993 or as Chomsky's (1986a) earlier rejection of theories that ensure through extra syntactic means, additional to FI, that structures of vacuous quantification are not generated. Consider for example (5) and (6):

(5) *Who did you see Bill

(6)   Who did you see t

Chomsky argues that since (5) is excluded at LF by an interpretive principle that rules out vacuous quantification—presumably a subcase of

FI—a theory with an additional syntactic mechanism to rule such examples out would be incorrect. Similarly, I would add, since there must be an LF concept (chain) or principle (Form Chain) to characterize the relationship between *who* and its trace in (6), a theory that provides an extra syntactic mechanism to do the same work is equally problematic.

Notice that this argument is one of conceptual economy, but it is different from the often-criticized erroneous conceptual economy argument against transformations. Thus Chomsky (1981, 90–92) explains that the rule of Move α is justified by the need to express a clustering of properties: certain relationships are constrained in a particular way by Subjacency, the ECP, and theta theory. Move α expresses these relations, which contrast with others such as construal or disjoint reference relations. In this connection, Chomsky discusses the difference between two theories, or two versions of the same theory. One of these incorporates the rule of Move α; the other rejects this rule and expresses the relevant relations by means of an interpretive principle. He cautions against the fallacy of preferring a theory without Move α on the grounds that this eliminates the class of transformational devices and thereby simplifies the theory. The argument from simplicity is erroneous since Move α would be eliminated only at the cost of introducing a new type of interpretive rule with exactly the properties of Move α.

But the present argument is different. I assume that the LF principle of Form Chain or the LF concept of chain relevant for the interpretation of antecedent-trace type relations is not a new type of entity but one that is necessary in any case, that is independently motivated (by FI). Thus eliminating Move α genuinely simplifies the theory. Trace theory made it possible in principle to eliminate movement transformations; FI provides reason to think that it is necessary to do so.

Finally, another simple consideration suggests strongly that the grammar needs to make use of the concept of chains. As discussed above, evidence for chains should automatically be taken as evidence against Move α, since Move α is an additional syntactic mechanism that characterizes the same relationships that chains capture. Consider the fact that movement always lands in a nonthematic position. We can state this in chain-theoretical terms as the principle that all non-root positions of chains are nonthematic (where the root of the chain is its most deeply embedded position). Let us call this generalization the Main Thematic Condition (MTC). In a theory where LF is the sole semantic interface, the notion of theta position is relevant only at LF and therefore the

MTC must hold here. But then the MTC must be a chain condition, since the output of a given application of Move α may or may not be LF. But the MTC as a condition on Move α would have to be a constraint on all Move α relations, not just on those that constitute the final step in the derivation leading to LF.

Notice that the consideration from the MTC, just like the one from FI, militates only against theories that have both representational principles and the rule of Move α. These arguments do not show by themselves that a fully representational theory with no derivational processes is preferable to a fully derivational one that has no single interpretive interface. However, they indicate that a theory that is restrictive enough to postulate the semantic interface level of LF, but additionally keeps derivational processes, is redundant and thus incorrect.

1.3 Explaining the MTC

In standard Principles and Parameters theory, the MTC has been attributed to the Theta Criterion's holding at both LF and D-structure (cf. Chomsky 1981, 1986a and Brody 1990a, 1993). Simplifying somewhat, the explanation went as follows. The D-structure Theta Criterion makes it necessary for an argument A to occupy a thematic position at this level. If A subsequently moves into another thematic position, then the LF Theta Criterion is violated: A's chain will have more than one theta position. In Brody 1990a and 1993 I argued that the explanation of the MTC based on the D-structure Theta Criterion is incorrect, primarily because there is no motivation for considering the Theta Criterion as a syntactic principle rather than as an interpretive requirement (see also Chomsky 1992). I suggested an explanation that derived the MTC from the Projection Principle. Recall that Chomsky's (1981) Projection Principle had two requirements: (a) syntactic structure is projected from the lexicon, and (b) every syntactic level should conform to the requirements of lexical projection. In a theory without derivations there would be only a single syntactic level, so condition (b) must be irrelevant. The status of condition (a), however, remains open.

Consider categorial projection first: a category of type X projects other (higher level) categories of the same type X. This phenomenon is restricted to taking place only in the root position of the chain of X. Call the set of chain-root positions of a structure its D-set (as in Brody, 1991b, 1993). Then (7) holds:

(7) Categorial projection is possible only in positions that belong to the
    D-set.

There are also certain lexical contextual conditions that always hold in
the D-set. The selectional requirements of a category C are invariably
valid only in the root position of the chain of C. It seems a natural step to
account for this by assuming that selection is also a matter of projection
and extending (7) to projection in general:

(8) Projectional requirements can hold only in positions that belong to
    the D-set.

Strictly speaking, (8) is not a syntactic principle, but a more general one
that has both syntactic and semantic effects. Thus it holds for selection in
general, including both syntactic (c-) selection and semantic (s-) selection.
Now let us return to the condition that all theta positions are chain-roots,
the MTC. In present terms we can state this as the requirement that thematic frames have to be satisfied by members of the D-set. But this will
follow from an immediate generalization of (8):

(9) *The Generalized Projection Principle (GPP)*:
    Projectional requirements can only involve positions that belong to
    the D-set.

Projectional requirements are restricted by (9) to hold in, and to be
satisfied by, D-set positions. Thus the MTC can be taken to be a consequence of the way certain aspects of the syntactic representation are
projected from the lexicon—that is, of the GPP.

    Consider the simplified example in (10):

(10) Mary$_x$ embrasse$_y$ t$_x$ t$_y$ Pierre
     M   kisses   P

    Take t$_x$ to be the VP-internal trace of the subject and t$_y$ to be that
of the verb. The GPP requires the verb *embrasse* to project categorially
and select from the root position of its chain t$_y$ and the DP *Mary* to
be selected in the root position of its chain t$_x$. It prevents this verb
from selecting or categorially projecting from the non-root position of
its chain (here VP-externally). And, crucially, the GPP also rules out
configurations in which the non-root position of a chain is in a selected
position, as in (11) and (12) (see chapter 3 for more discussion of such
cases):

(11) *John$_x$ hit t$_x$

(12) *John$_x$ believes t$_x$ to seem that S

Extending the principle that restricts projectional requirements to root positions of chains in (8) to the GPP leads to a problem, however. The additional requirement of the GPP, that projectional features must always be satisfied by chain roots, appears to be violated by categorial features. In the case of non-roots of XP-chains, the categorial feature (of the head of XP) seems to be assignable to a position (that of the XP) that does not belong to the D-set of the sentence. We can avoid this conclusion if we distinguish categories and positions and assume that while selectional features are assigned to categories through the positions they occupy, categorial features simply project categories, ignoring their positions. Both categorial and selectional features would continue to be assigned through the position of the assigner. The GPP will then require selectional and categorial projection to hold and selection to be satisfied in root positions, as desired. (An alternative approach to this problem is provided by the copy theory of chains; cf. chapter 5 below for discussion.) If traces are copies—or at least "layered"—then we could assume that categorial projection in fact always takes place in the root positions of XP-chains. Categorial features of the maximal projection on which the chain is formed can then percolate up the chain—in cases of "overt movement" along with other properties of the root element.)

The GPP thus entails the MTC, but this raises the next question: Why should the GPP itself hold? So far I have assumed that projectional features express relations between syntactic positions, perhaps apart from categorial projection, which I took to be a relation between a position and a category or set of categories. Suppose, however, that selectional feature projection is not a relation between syntactic positions but a relation between chains, and similarly that categorial projection involves a relation between a chain and a category. We can then take a selectional feature P to be saturated only if it identifies all positions in a chain C. Take a position to be so identified if it carries (a copy of) P. This means that P must spread from the position where it is assigned to all members of the assignee chain C. Similarly, suppose that satisfaction of the projectional feature P (where P may be either a selectional or a categorial feature) must also spread to all members of the (head-)chain that assigns P. A possible way of executing this requirement would be to assume that all members of the assigner chain carry P, the projectional feature of their lexical element, and satisfaction of P results in assigning some feature S to P. S must then spread to the instance of P on each member of the assigner chain. Now the GPP will follow from the assumption that feature percolation in chains is always bottom to top; there is no "feature lowering." The principle required is thus the representational equivalent of the ban on lowering transformations of the derivational framework.

To see how this explanation works in concrete cases, consider again the MTC violation in (11) and (12) where the chain [John,t] contains a selected non-root position. Given the ban on feature lowering, the theta role assigned to the non-root position cannot spread to the position of the trace. It will thus fail to identify all positions of the chain, leaving the theta role unsaturated. In the case of a head chain, if categorial projection or selection took place from the non-root position, then the feature S indicating the satisfaction of this requirement again could not percolate to the copy of the projectional feature in the position of the trace of the head, leaving the projectional features there unsaturated.

There is a loophole in the above argument that might need to be closed. The explanation assumes that a selectional feature on a member of a head chain can be satisfied in two distinct ways. It may be satisfied directly, by assignment to (all members of) some chain, or indirectly, through the upward percolation of the satisfaction feature. The prohibition on feature lowering restricts direct satisfaction to the root position in general, but not yet in all cases. The account still allows a projectional feature P to be directly satisfied in a non-root position provided that the same feature also holds and is directly satisfied in the root position of the assigner chain. In such a configuration, if P was saturated in both positions then all instances of P in the assigner chain could be S-marked. We could close this loophole by requiring that a projectional feature associated with a chain C can be directly satisfied only in a single position in C, perhaps as an instance of a general property of checking features.

On the other hand, Pesetsky (1992) argues that precisely such configurations occur: in certain cases head chains can directly select the same XP chain in two distinct positions. If he is correct, then the requirement that projectional features can hold only in a unique position in a chain could be dispensed with. (Note that in such configurations it will also be the case that the selectional feature is assigned to the XP chain in more than one position, only one of which is the root of the chain. But all positions in the XP-chain would be marked by this feature as required.) This move would create some further technical problems. It will then be necessary to ensure that a selectional feature that is directly satisfied in more than one position is satisfied in all positions by assignment to the same chain. (Similarly, a categorial feature that is directly satisfied in more than one position would presumably have to be satisfied by the same category, with the result that this option would not be available for categorial projection at all.)

However this issue of uniqueness is resolved, the GPP can be attributed to the representational incarnation of the "no lowering" principle. As we have seen, given certain not unnatural assumptions the prohibition against feature lowering entails the restriction of the projectional features to the D-set. But, crucially, no similar result can be obtained in a derivational framework from prohibiting lowering applications of Move α. Excluding lowering rules does not seem to help explain why raising into selected, selecting, or categorially projecting positions is invariably impossible (at least apart from the well-definable set of cases just noted). This, then, provides a further argument for chains and thus against Move α. (For discussions of Chomsky's (1994) recent conspiracy account of the MTC and of the other main effects of the GPP, see Brody 1994, van de Koot 1994.)

The conclusion that there are no movement transformations within syntax comes very close to a theory that has only one syntactic level of representation and no syntactic derivation (apart from lexical insertion). Notice that I am using the concept of "level of representation" here in the standard sense, a special case of the more general concept of linguistic level. One can think of a linguistic level abstractly, as an entity motivated by exhibiting its own primitives and axioms. In this sense, the modules of the Principles and Parameters theory also define levels. But I am of course not using level of representation in this general sense. If there is a (transformational) mapping between the lexical input and the interface level, LF, then this mapping may have intermediate stages where conditions must hold. To the extent that this is the case, we have syntactic levels additional to LF, in the usual, more specific sense.

Eliminating movement rules comes close to eliminating Affect α, although the question of the existence of deletion remains. In other words it comes close to showing that there is no transformational mapping between the lexical input and LF. If there is no such mapping then of course it can have no intermediate stages and therefore there can be no levels of representation other than LF.

In the next section I shall argue that it is not unreasonable to adopt the radical view in general and explore a theory without derivations. A nonderivational Principles and Parameters theory has been put forward by Koster (1987). (See also Koster 1978.) One of my main conclusions in this volume appears to be identical to one of his main conclusions: there are no movement rules in syntax. But this appearance is somewhat misleading, since the two theories are quite different. Koster (1987) rejects the claim that there is a cluster of properties uniquely characterizing certain relations expressed in standard Principles and Parameters theory by Move α and proposes his Thesis of Radical Autonomy: "the core properties of grammar are construction independent." While this might well be true on some appropriate level of abstraction, the claim that the relations expressed standardly by Move α form a natural class of core grammar, readily characterizable in terms of the usual clustering of properties (ECP, Subjacency, and the relevant Case and thematic conditions) remains convincing to me. Thus while Koster rejects the hypothesis that there is a special type of relation expressed by Move α, my claim is different and weaker: I propose that Move α is not the appropriate way of expressing this relation. Still, the theory presented here (like the one in Brody 1991b, 1993) of course shares the assumption with both Koster 1987 and Chomsky 1993 that there is only a single syntactic level, i.e., a single level between the lexical input and interpretation, at which representational principles can apply.

1.4 Lexico-Logical Form

In standard Principles and Parameters theory, Move α (or Affect α) relates lexical input to LF, the interface with the central conceptual systems. In the standard version of the theory lexical input is organized into a level of representation, D-structure. But since it is necessary for the lexicon and our post-LF interpretive apparatus to interact, it would clearly be desirable in principle for them to do so directly. Rather than relate the lexical input to a distinct interface level through a transformational mapping, we should, if possible, have the lexicon constrain LF directly and more strongly: have lexical insertion/projection take place at LF.

This argument could in principle be repeated also for the pair of interface levels LF, PF. But of course even though abstractly it might be desirable to have a common sensory/motor and conceptual interface, it would appear to be the case that such a direct interface does not exist.

The principles of PF organization and the elements they operate on seem to be of a very different nature and completely disjoint from the principles and primitives of LF. We consequently assume that there must be two distinct levels related by some mapping. However, no similar situation is encountered in the case of the lexical input and LF. The concepts and principles taken to be necessary to characterize the presentation of lexical material to syntax at D-structure (essentially X′- and theta-theory) are a subset of the principles necessary to characterize LF. Thus there is no general empirical difficulty in taking the lexicon to constrain LF directly, and no difficulty in assuming that the presentation of lexical material takes place at LF.

There is a curious feature of the organization of syntax shared by all versions of Principles and Parameters theory that include movement transformations and interface conditions, including variants as different as, for example, those of Williams (1986) and Chomsky (1993). In these frameworks there will inevitably be a large number of classes of pre-LF representations that correspond to no well-formed LF configurations. Whenever a derivation violates only some LF principle, a set of pre-LF representations (S-structures and pre-S-structure subtrees in the standard minimalist framework, S- and D-structures in earlier versions of the theory) will have been generated. Such massive overgeneration of structures is unavoidable in a transformational syntax with output conditions. This consideration would also seem to favour a nonderivational syntax that can provide a more elegant system of interaction between the lexicon and our conceptual systems. Notice that the issue here is not generative capacity but theoretical elegance.

I am proposing, then, to adopt a theory where there is only a single syntactic interface level, a level that both the lexicon and the conceptual systems have access to. I shall call this level of representation Lexico-Logical Form (LLF), where the distinction with standard LF representations is relevant. Otherwise I shall continue to use the term "LF," keeping in mind that a different status is now attributed to this level. LLF still needs to be related to the interface of sensory and motor systems, PF. I shall refer to the theory incorporating these assumptions the Lexico-Logical Form theory. (Cf. Brody 1985, 1987 for the first suggestions that the basic level of representation is LF and Brody 1991a, 1991b, 1992 for an earlier version of the LLF theory.)

The assumption that D-structure is a substructure of another level has often been discussed and sometimes been adopted (Sportiche 1983; Rizzi

1986a; Koster 1987). Koster also appears to view D-structure as a set of positions, rather than as a hierarchical structure. In these discussions the level on which D-structure is determined is taken to be S-structure. My proposal here and its earlier versions of computing D-sets from LF representations is different in that it takes (L)LF to be the basic syntactic level of representation. This makes the claim that the basic level is the interface level. The proposal differs also in more directly empirical ways, since it takes various properties of this interface to be different from those of S-structure (see section 7 and chapter 5 below).

The status of S-structure, understood as the input to phonology potentially distinct from LF, raises a further conceptual issue. Most versions of the standard framework (including again the minimalist theory) assume that in the derivations between lexical input and LF there is a point, not necessarily identical to LF, that relays information to PF. But this idea seems less appealing once we move away from the intuitively satisfying picture of a syntactic representation (S-structure) interpreted quasi-semantically and phonologically to a theory where the mapping between lexical input and LF is essentially uniform and contrasts with a distinct phonological system. It then becomes rather unclear why the input to PF should be a point that is distinct from LF. The syntactic derivation has to do with the relation between LF and lexical items and properties; one would not expect this relation to enter directly into the LF-PF mapping. Just as in earlier versions of GB theory the input to PF rules was not taken to precede S-structure, in a theory with a uniform syntactic mapping between the lexical input and LF one would expect PF to spell out the level that contains the semantic/cognitive interface representation, rather than some arbitrary point (S-structure) in the derivation.

Consider the status of S-structure within the LLF theory. Here S-structure in the standard sense cannot exist. There cannot be an intermediate point on the derivation between lexical input and LF, since such a derivation is not part of the grammar. The mapping, which following standard minimalist terminology I shall call "SPELLOUT," relates LLF to PF. This is not because SPELLOUT is arbitrarily restricted to apply only at LLF, but because the theory contains no syntactic derivations (apart from lexical insertion), no transformational mapping between lexical input and (L)LF. There is only one syntactic structure, LLF, so this must be the input to SPELLOUT. Since the theory has no movement, categories in LLF representations will have to occupy their PF positions.

Note that the argument against taking an S-structure that need not be identical to LF as the input to SPELLOUT is not that a representational theory will necessarily predict the position of the lexical elements or that it necessarily has a simpler system in this domain. Just as in the derivational theory some principle P will determine which point in a given derivation is the input to SPELLOUT, in the LLF approach some principle P′ will be responsible for establishing where lexical categories will be in their chain (see section 1.7 and chapter 4 below). The point of the argument is different: computations that have to do with P/P′ have to do with the relation between lexical properties and (L)LF structures. They seem irrelevant to and therefore should not directly enter into the (L)LF-PF mapping. By assuming that the overt position of categories is an LLF property, the P/P′-related complexity can be placed at LLF and the (L)LF-PF mapping can be accordingly simplified. SPELLOUT can thus be taken to map the undistorted semantic/cognitive interface level to PF.

The nonderivational nature of the theory entails that LLF representations will generally be like S-structures in the standard Principles and Parameters theory with respect to the positions lexical categories occupy (but see chapter 5). These LLF representations will, however, also be significantly different not only from the S-structures of the standard Principles and Parameters theory but also from the various enriched S-structures of some other related theories, for example those of Williams 1986 or Koster 1987. As noted earlier, in contrast to Koster I make the standard assumption that relations that are usually expressed by movement form a natural class. The claim here is only that the appropriate way of expressing these relations is not by Move α but by (LLF) chains. As opposed to Williams's theory, under the present proposal this class will include both overt and LF "movement" relations (see section 1.7). Since expressing both overt and covert chains is a crucial property—perhaps *the* crucial property—distinguishing (L)LF from S-structure, the proposals put forward here will differ from Williams's theory in the way the terminology suggests: he argued for S-structure and I argue for (L)LF.

1.5 Minimalist Theories

Chomsky (1993) proposes in his "minimalist program" that conditions on representations may hold only at the interface levels of LF and PF and that legitimate constraints must be motivated by properties of the interface, "perhaps properly understood as modes of interpretation by performance systems" (Chomsky 1993, 4). He argues convincingly for restricting conditions on representations to the interface levels. If the project of restricting syntactic representational conditions to LF can be successfully carried out, it will of course vindicate the claim that LF is the basic level of representation (Brody 1985, 1987, 1991a). The assumption that LF is the only syntactic level appears also in Brody 1991b (where S-structure is taken to be an intermediate point on the LF-to-PF mapping).

Chomsky proposes further that "linguistic expressions are the optimal realizations of the interface conditions, where 'optimality' is determined by the economy conditions of UG" (Chomsky 1993, 4). The economy conditions fall naturally into two classes: economy of representations and economy of derivation. FI can be taken as a main representant of the former category. Economy principles constraining derivations include principles that require derivations to have the smallest number of steps and the shortest possible ones. This theory is like the standard framework in that here also Move α relates lexical input to LF, the interface with the central conceptual systems. In the standard Principles and Parameters theory, lexical input is organized into a level of representation, D-structure. In the minimalist approach, elements drawn from the lexicon project disjoint X′-subtrees, that are to be joined eventually by the generalized transformation, GT. Chomsky appears to assume that lexical contextual requirements hold at LF but explicitly states that X′-projection of categories can precede the application of GT. The X′-structures projected by the lexical heads are composed into a joint (first S-structure and then LF) representation by GT. Move α is another way in which GT can apply.

Recall the argument against the standard framework in the previous section: since it is necessary for the lexicon and our central cognitive processes to interact, optimally this interaction should be direct, not mediated through a transformational mapping. This requirement has a weaker and a stronger form. The weaker version is that (a) the lexicon should constrain LF directly, and the stronger one that (b) lexical insertion/projection should take place at LF.

Chomsky generally adopts the view that lexical constraints hold only at LF (and PF), but maintains that lexical elements enter syntax prior to S-structure. Thus, apart from the assumption that X′-theory holds where lexical items are presented, his theory appears to satisfy the weaker of the two requirements but not the stronger one: the lexicon constrains LF directly but lexical insertion takes place elsewhere. The assumption that X'-theory holds where lexical items are presented is problematic in the minimalist framework, where constraints on representations should hold only at LF. Chomsky refers to pre-LF X'-theory as the "sole residue of the Projection Principle," but this only gives a name to the problem. It would appear that within his minimalist theory, projection should be taken to be free at this stage, X'-theory violations being filtered only at LF. This would make the treatment of the X'-constraints parallel to the treatment of the thematic component: LF filtering of structures composed by GT that do not satisfy theta theory.

The question of where X'-theory holds perhaps highlights the lack of elegance in the standard minimalist approach, a problem inherent in all derivational systems with output conditions. In this framework, perhaps even more than in others, most syntactic derivations will generate useless structures (structures that are input to SPELLOUT, pre-LF–post-SPELLOUT trees and pre-SPELLOUT subtrees) to be discarded at the LF level. Notice that the problem is specific to derivational theories and is not one that will arise in any modular theory. In a modular theory, structures that violate only one module will be accepted in all other modules. But it is not necessarily the case that there will be intermediate structures accepted by some subtheory waiting to be excluded by some other. In a theory where all constraints can apply simultaneously there need not be such intermediate structures. Thus the problem of over-generation of intermediate structures arises from having separate levels, not from the modularity of the grammar.

In the standard minimalist theory all representational constraints hold at the interface levels. Chomsky states also that only the interface levels exist, which is inevitably true if it is a necessary condition of X's being a level of representation that some representational conditions hold at X. But in a derivational theory an infinite number of non-interface structures are generated by applications of lexical insertion and GT. These structures do not qualify, then, as levels of representation; no representational conditions can be stated on them. The LLF theory provides an explanation of why no conditions can hold on these structures: it is because they do not exist. LLF representations are generated directly from the lexicon, all lexical insertion taking place in one step. The LLF theory is then radically minimalist: there can be only interface representational conditions, since within syntax only the interface structure exists.

Let me add here two general observations concerning some of the derivational principles in this theory. Take, first, the extension requirement on GT. In essence this ensures that GT assembles the syntactic representation in a strictly cyclic fashion. Postulating a condition with the effect of the cycle is problematic, however, in a minimalist theory. Either the cycle operates only in overt syntax or it has to restart after S-structure, since LF-movement can apply in embedded domains. In either case we would have an S-structure property, contrary to minimalist assumptions.

Chomsky bases the extension requirement on the following consideration: the economy condition of the shortest move will derive Relativized Minimality effects only if the intervening element is inserted before movement across its position is attempted. Clearly, in the fully representational LLF theory the cycle would be unnecessary to achieve such effects. The equivalent of the shortest-move requirement (make chain-links the shortest possible) will apply correctly, since both the antecedent and the intervener are necessarily present simultaneously. (See chapter 5 for an alternative to the extension requirement in the account of reconstruction structures.)

Recently Chomsky (1994), noting the stipulative nature of the extension condition, has proposed its elimination. He suggests making the shortest-move requirement sensitive also to "the 'potential specifier' of F [a functional head] with a DP-feature along with actual (filled) SPEC; thus neither SPEC nor a head with a DP-feature can be 'skipped' in a derivation" (Chomsky 1994, 24). Further assumptions entail that the relevant DP-features are the strong ones. But the disjunction of DP-features and SPECs or actual and potential SPECs appears to miss the obvious representational generalization that it seems to be designed to describe.

Consider next the principles of "shortest move" and "fewest derivational steps." These are easily restatable representationally, as preferences for the shortest and/or fewest chain-links. But as Chomsky notes, there is a conflict between these two principles. The shorter the moves, the greater the number of steps in the derivation. Similarly, shorter chain-links entail more of them. Chomsky suggests that "[t]he paradox is resolved if we take the basic transformational operation to be not Move α but *Form Chain*" (Chomsky 1993, 15). Given this operation, a chain that corresponds to several successive applications of Move α to the same element would be formed in a single step. (Note that this proposal is different from the one put forward above, according to which chains make derivations redundant. Chomsky's point appears to be only that several successive applications of Move α to the same element count as a single unit and thus as a single step in the derivation.) This solution resolves the conflict by eliminating much of the content of the "fewest steps" principle. Still the restriction seems to be natural and desirable. The LLF theory captures the spirit of this principle which requires derivations to contain the smallest possible number of steps, in a radical way. Within the nonderivational LLF theory the number of steps is constantly zero (or one), so the LLF theory can be taken to incorporate a principle of radical derivational economy.

1.6   The Status of D-Structure

In the standard minimalist theory D-structure does not exist. Lexical items are presented to syntax in an X′ format independently of each other, and these X′ subtrees are combined into a unitary phrase marker by a generalized transformation GT. Move α is a subcase of GT.

The standard minimalist framework dispenses with D-structure in a manner both stronger and weaker than that of the LLF theory (or Brody 1991b, 1993). It is stronger since it completely dispenses with D-structure as an entity defined by the grammar, whereas within LLF theory the concept of D-set is defined (as the set of chain-roots); all lexical projectional requirements must hold there. Some concept like the D-set appears necessary to describe and account for the MTC. Chomsky's (1993) theory, rejecting the concept of a grammar-internal entity through which lexical projection of syntactic structures takes place, provides no explanation, as he notes. But the LLF theory's elimination of D-structure is also stronger than Chomsky's. As we have seen, the standard minimalist theory maintains that there is a derivation, potentially including applications of Move α, between the lexical input to syntax (which is not organized into a level of representation) and the conceptual interface LF. The radically minimalist LLF theory denies this, asserting instead that LLF representations are created from the lexical input in one step.

Chomsky provides three arguments against a level of D-structure. Let us check whether these arguments are problematic for our concept of D-set. First, he notes that D-structure cannot be formed from an unordered set of elements from the lexicon; "... different arrangements of lexical items will yield different expressions" (Chomsky 1993, 20). Thus the matter of how lexical items are organized into a D-structure needs to be clarified. Whatever force this observation has against standard D-structure (or against the present proposal of projecting LF directly from the lexicon), clearly it is irrelevant for the matter of D-sets, since D-sets do not need to be ordered.

Second, the standard framework "requires conditions to ensure that D-structure has basic properties of LF.... The Projection Principle and the Theta Criterion have no independent significance at LF." "If they are not met, the expression receives some deviant interpretation at the interface." "But at D-structure, the two principles are needed to make the picture coherent.... These principles are therefore dubious on conceptual grounds, though it remains to account for their empirical consequences, such as the constraint against substitution into a Θ-position" (Chomsky 1993, 20). These arguments are similar or identical to the ones put forward independently in Brody 1993, with respect to the Theta Criterion. As for the Projection Principle, recall that this consists of two conditions: first, the syntactic representation must be projected from the lexicon; second, the lexical requirements involved should be satisfied at every level. The second condition has to be rejected within the standard minimalist theory, where conditions may hold only at the interface level. It is also excluded in principle within the radically minimalist LLF theory, where there is only a single syntactic structure. The first condition, that syntactic representations are projected from the lexicon, is an interface condition, perfectly legitimate within a minimalist theory. It was motivated as an expression of the pervasive generalization that lexical projection operates in the D-set, an operation of which one consequence is the MTC.

Third, Chomsky argues that adjectival complement constructions of the *easy to please* type pose an empirical problem for the standard concept of D-structure. In constructions like (13) there is evidence for the presence of an empty operator. "The evidence for the S-structure [(13)] is compelling, but *John* occupies a non Θ-position and hence cannot appear at D-structure" (Chomsky 1993, 21).

(13) John is easy [Op [PRO to please t]]

However, the conclusion follows from the premise only under the assumption that movement from A'- to A-position is prohibited. In Brody 1990a and 1993 I argued that this hypothesis should be dropped and that

(13) is best analyzed as involving the (A-A'-A) chain [John,Op,t]. The construction thus creates no significant problem even for the standard conception of D-structure. In movement terms (13) should be analyzed as involving movement of the NP *John* from embedded object position to spec of CP and then to the matrix subject position. In spec of CP it would leave behind a trace that is eventually interpreted as an operator.

I conclude, then, that Chomsky provides only one strong argument against D-structure, the same one given independently in Brody 1993: the postulation of D-structure in the standard framework involves the hypothesis that constraints like the Theta Criterion hold at the D-structure level. But it is dubious to extend in this way LF constraints that are motivated by virtue of the interpretation of that level. As we have seen, D-sets, whose existence is motivated by the MTC, are immune to this criticism. In LLF theory D-sets are included in LF; they are part of the conceptual interface.

Some theories that assume binary branching trees might appear to conflict with the postulation of D-sets. Consider, for example, Larson's (1988) analysis of the VP, in the context of the definition of minimal complement domain in Chomsky 1992. Under Larson's analysis, a sentence like (14) will contain a VP like (15) at D-structure:

(14) Mary put the book on the shelf

(15)

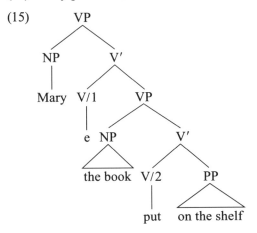

The verb *put* is then taken to raise to V/1 before any further raising into some higher head node takes place. (I assume that subject and object are also chain-related, through overt or LF raising in the derivational framework, to some higher spec position.) The problem that arises here is identifying the complements of the verb, finding the definition that can distinguish these from its specifier, the subject.

Chomsky's concept of minimal complement domain appears useful for this purpose. Given his definitions, not only the category [*put*], but also the chain [put,t] has a minimal complement domain. Essentially, the minimal complement domain of the chain is the smallest set of nodes S such that (*a*) its members dominate all nodes dominated by the complement of the head of the chain, and (*b*) no member of S dominates those nodes that contain some other member of the chain. Thus the minimal complement domain of [put,t] is the NP *the book* and the PP *on the shelf*, the categories that are the complements of the verb under the earlier ternary branching analysis.

Identifying the complements of a head with the minimal complement domain of its chain does not, strictly speaking, contradict the generalization that projectional (thematic, X′-labeling, etc.) features can only be assigned in the root positions of chains. Once (minimal) complement (domain) is defined with respect to the chain, the complements are then selected from the root position, in accordance with the generalization developed in section 1.3.

It may be argued, however, that the spirit of the generalization is violated: the case is unique in that information from a non-root chain-position is necessary for proper selection. Note, first, that not all binary branching analyses create this problem. No such difficulty would arise, for example, under Pesetsky's (1992) cascade structure analysis of the same phenomena. Another alternative would be not to consider the direct object *the book* in (15) the complement of the chain [put,t] at all. This puts in question the status of the subject *Mary*: if the direct object is really the spec of the verb, what is the subject? Perhaps one could postulate an empty morpheme that assigns the agent theta role to the subject. The verb *put* with this morpheme would be related to *put* without it as *melt* in "John melted the ice" is to *melt* in "The ice melted" (cf. Koizumi 1993 for a similar suggestion made independently). An approach along these lines would also resolve the X′-labeling problem of the higher VP. If we assume that this XP is a VP as a consequence of V raising into it, then again we have a violation of the major generalization that projectional features hold only in the D-set. On the other hand, a verbal morpheme whose chain-root position will be the head of this VP will label this projection appropriately.

Although Chomsky considers V/1 in (15) to be an "empty position," postulating a higher verb of this sort appears necessary even within his system of assumptions. If there is no higher VP-internal V head in (15) for the lower verb *put* to move to, then further movement of *put* (say to spec-AGRO) will incorrectly extend the minimal complement domain of the chain of this verb to include the subject *Mary*. Given the higher V head, further movement to some next-higher head would involve this category and not the lower verb, creating a separate chain and thus avoiding the unwanted consequence. (A similar conclusion that V/1 must be a "light verb" appears in Chomsky 1994. His considerations also have to do with what I would take to be effects of the GPP. See Brody 1994 for further discussion.)

1.7 "LF-Movement" in the LLF Theory

I have argued that the grammar contains no movement rules: FI makes the concept of chains necessary, but chains make movement rules redundant. The theory that incorporates them is therefore incorrect. The argument from FI holds quite generally. It entails not only that Move α does not exist in syntax, but also that SPELLOUT, the LF-PF mapping, contains no movement rules either. In other words, it follows that at LF lexical material must not be in a position different from where we observe it at PF.

What about the LF movement rules of the standard framework? In general we can express these dependencies by chains in which the category that is standardly taken to move covertly is not in the highest position. Take the rule of Expletive Replacement:

(16) There arrived a man

(17) a. Many people must have arrived
       b. There must have arrived many people

The expletive argument association in (16) ([there, a man]) is similar to movement rules in that it appears to be constrained by the strict locality requirement(s), the MTC, and the Case-theoretical principles characteristic of these. Agreement properties (the possibility of "subject-verb agreement" with the postverbal associate) and the option of extending the relation through movement of the expletive (e.g., as in "There seems t to have arrived the man") reinforce this conclusion.

Expressing the generalization in terms of movement is problematic, however. If (17b) involves LF movement, then its LF representation will not be different from that of (17a). But in these cases the familiar scopal ambiguity exhibited by the overt movement constructions is missing (Williams 1984). Thus in (17b) *must* has higher scope than *many people*, while in (17a) either scope relation is possible. Chomsky's (1991, 1992) theory of LF adjunction of the associate to the expletive, where the expletive is considered an "LF-affix," takes account of this. But we can avoid the somewhat dubious notion of LF-affix by assuming that the "movement" properties of expletive-associate dependencies are those of chains. Having dispensed with LF movement here, we can then determine scopal relations by the LF/surface positions of the quantificational elements. The assumption that an element can have scope over whatever it m-commands suffices to account for the cases at hand: *must* and *many people* m-command each other in (17a), while in (17b) the auxiliary asymmetrically m-commands this quantificational NP.

What about Full Interpretation, the principle that Chomsky (1991) takes to make replacement of the expletive *there* obligatory? Recall that other chain-internal expletives (adjunct- head- and NP-traces) must be present at LF. The generalization I proposed earlier was that FI applies chain externally. This automatically allows expletives like *it* and *there* to be present at LLF. Indeed, they could be ruled out by FI only at the cost of introducing additional, apparently unmotivated complexity.

To accommodate these structures, chains that contain more than one lexical category must be allowed. Assume that such A-chains are constructible in principle, but excluded in all cases where an argument is associated with a nonexpletive category. If an A-chain is taken to be an abstract representation of the argument it contains (Chomsky 1986a), then an A-chain with more than one argument will be uninterpretable (Brody 1993).

Overt expletives can be found not only in the covert NP-movement case but also in covert head and A′-movement constructions. For example, the article *il* in the Italian (18b) has been argued by Longobardi (1992) to be an expletive introducing the head noun. Similarly the default scope indicator wh-word *was* in the German partial Wh-movement construction (18c) (McDaniel 1989) appears to be a lexical expletive associated with the contentful wh-phrase. Perhaps the *do* of do-support in (18a) can also be taken to be an expletive associated with a contentful verb (Manzini 1992b).

(18) a. John didn't come
   b. Il mio Gianni ha telefonato
      The my G   called
   c. Was hat Hans gesagt wer ist gekommen
      'What did H say who came,' i.e., Who did H say came

This suggests that the treatment of expletive-argument structures should be generalized to all LF-movement constructions. Assume, in other words, that covert movement structures are analyzed as expletive-associate chains, where the expletive may or may not have phonological features. Thus, for example, in covert English "verb raising" and "Wh-raising" structures, I assume an empty expletive to be present, forming an LLF chain with the verb and the wh-in-situ, respectively:

(19) a. John e_x often comes$_x$ late
   b. [e_x Who] t saw what$_x$

In the case of wh-in-situ, the expletive functions as a scope-marking element. Likewise, Riemsdijk (1983) and Koster (1987), for example, assume that a scope-marker empty category is associated with wh-in-situ. Aoun and Li (1993) and Watanabe (1991) also postulate S-structure representations in which an empty scope-marking operator is associated with those wh-in-situ in Chinese and Japanese that correspond to the moved wh-phrase in English, although neither assumes that this operator forms a chain with the wh-in-situ. (As for the derivational status of this operator, Aoun and Li assume that it may and Watanabe that it must undergo movement. For the account of the ECP effects given by Aoun and Li this is not crucial. The intermediate traces needed in their approach could equally well have been "base generated," created at LLF by the operation of Form Chain. Watanabe, however, argues that the relation between the operator and the wh-in-situ is subject to Subjacency and that this is due to pre-S-structure movement of the empty operator. See chapter 2 below for discussion.) "Covert NP-movement" can be analyzed in the same fashion, as an expletive-associate chain. I assume that a similar treatment is appropriate for all other LF-movement relations that involve some form of spec-head licensing. (For a recent treatment of negation in these terms see Haegeman [forthcoming]. On Quantifier raising see chapter 4 below.)

Expletives, empty or not, contribute to the interpretation only minimally, if at all. Perhaps they can carry no lexically specified contribution to the interpretation; that is, whatever meaning component they appear to have is a property of the construction they appear in. Let us refer to nonexpletives as "contentives." More precisely, contentives are elements with substantive lexical contribution to meaning (cf. Brody 1985 for a related use of the term). Contentives will include phrasal arguments, heads, and operators (but not variables, in the syntactic sense). Generalizing further the treatment of expletive-argument structures, take chains to be the abstract representation of the contentive they contain. Chain construction can then in principle involve any number of lexical elements, but only a single contentive.

In the LLF theory, as in the standard frameworks, a chain will relate two positions, independently of whether the relation is of the overt or LF-movement type. The most salient difference between LF and overt movement, of course, has to do with the position of the "moved" contentive category. In the present framework, "overt movement" from position P/2 to position P/1 corresponds to a chain where the contentive is in P/1, and "LF movement" to a chain where it is in P/2. Thus the distinction between overt and LF movement, as it concerns the surface position of the "moved" material, translates in the present theory into the question of the chain-internal distribution of the contentive and the expletive(s). I return to some related problems in chapter 4, where I argue that far from being a notational variant of the standard view, the approach outlined here has significant advantages.

The present proposals agree with Williams (1986) as to the position of the contentive elements at the interface level. Thus the theory of expletive-associate chains could be viewed as an attempt to resolve empirical difficulties with Williams's view that S-structure is the input to interpretation, in other words that S-structure is the syntactic interface. But as noted earlier, this would be a misleading way of characterizing the proposal, which makes it possible to capture both overt and covert movement at one syntactic level. Expressing both overt and covert movement in terms of chains is a basic property of LF that has never been associated with S-structure, and one that crucially distinguishes LF from S-structure. (In particular, Williams's S-structure expresses quantification and reconstruction structures but not the standard cases of covert A- and A-bar movement.) Hence I will continue to refer to the interface level as (L)LF.

Let us finally consider an alternative way of expressing the scope of wh-in-situ: through coindexing with the appropriate wh-phrase in A'-

position, like Williams's (1986) treatment of QR. For example, matrix scope of *what* in (20a) could be indicated as in (20b).

(20) a. Who wondered whether John bought what
      b. Who$_{x,y}$ t$_x$ wondered whether John bought what$_y$

Such indexed structures have an apparent advantage: phenomena captured in the standard framework by the assumption that overt and LF movement have different properties are expected under this view; scopal annotation expresses a different relation from overt movement. The relevant phenomenon is Subjacency: according to a widely held view, Subjacency constrains only overt movement. The indexing theory makes it possible to dispense with this strange and undesirable restriction: all movement (but no scopal annotation) is constrained by Subjacency.

A similar view is presented in Chomsky 1993. He suggests that "[t]he LF rule that associates the in-situ *wh*-phrase with the *wh*-phrase in [SPEC, CP] need not be construed as an instance of Move α. We might think of it as the syntactic basis for absorption in the sense of Higginbotham and May (1981), an operation that associates two *wh*-phrases to form a generalized quantifier. If so, then the LF rule need satisfy none of the conditions on movement" (Chomsky 1993, 26). Chomsky expands on wh-phrase association in a footnote to this text: "The technical implementation could be developed in many ways. For now, let us think of it as a rule of interpretation for the paired *wh*-phrases." His view here is not essentially different in type from Williams's indexing theory of wh-in-situ. The main evidence would have to be the same in both cases: properties that are standardly attributed to overt movement but which its postulated LF counterpart does not share.

As already noted before, it is quite problematic to consider the relation expressed in the standard framework by Wh-raising to differ from the one standardly expressed by overt Wh-movement. The overt and the LF-movement rules of the standard framework share certain crucial properties. In particular, they are both subject to the ECP and the MTC. Within these theories, the phenomena captured by the similarity of overt and LF- (wh-) movement are unexpected. Additionally, I argue in chapter 2 that the evidence for such theories is spurious, and adduce further evidence for the claim that Subjacency also constrains relations expressed standardly by LF-movement. If this is the case, then there remains no motivation for expressing the LF-movement of the standard framework by some mechanism (like annotation or some other

interpretive rule) different from the one that captures overt-movement-
type relations.

In the theory proposed here, overt-movement–type relations are expressed by the concept of chains. If the foregoing considerations are
correct, then covert-movement–type relations, that is, expletive-contentive ones (including "Wh-raising"), are also chain relations. The MTC,
the ECP, and (as we shall see) Subjacency remain conditions on chains.

1.8 Conclusion

In sections 1.1 through 1.3 of this chapter I argued against the rule of
Move α. The concept of chains is necessary at LF, but given chains the
concept of Move α is redundant. Chains are made necessary by FI and the
MTC. Chains and not categories must be the elements to which the principle of FI applies, otherwise certain traces would violate FI. Because the
MTC involves the LF notion of theta position it can only apply at this
level, and therefore must apply to chains rather than to Move α. The explanation of the MTC and of the more inclusive GPP proposed here also
crucially exploits the notion of chains.

These considerations led to a theory of grammar that contains no
movement rules and no derivations in the usual sense: (L)LF representations are projected from the lexicon in one step. The SPELLOUT
rule that operates between syntactic representations and PF ones can
apply only to this level, since not only are there no other syntactic levels
of representation, there are no intermediate structures of any kind.

An additional argument against syntactic derivation (and thus for
assembling LF in one step), derives from a general consideration of
theoretical elegance. A system in which the lexicon has direct access to
(L)LF avoids the problem of generating a large number of ill formed
syntactic structures that must be filtered at the later interface stage.

In sections 1.5 through 1.7 I compared the LLF approach to the
standard minimalist theory. The general advantages claimed for the
former included the following: (*a*) The arguments from the redundancy
of Move α and from the theoretical inelegance of overgeneration of intermediate structures apply to any framework where the lexicon does
not interface directly with the conceptual-interpretive system, hence also
to the (non-radically) minimalist view. (b) Only the *radically* minimalist
theory can strongly explain why no constraints hold at non-interface
structures: because they do not exist. (c) The minimalist (but not the

radically minimalist) theory exhibits the conceptually curious design where a subset of the computations involved in the assembly of LF from the lexical input must be part of the LF-PF mapping.

I also suggested that LF movement should be analysed in terms of LLF chains that involve expletive-contentive relations. Chapters 2 and 4 contain further arguments for this proposal.

1.9 Appendix 1

Chomsky (1987) sketches three arguments against an earlier version of the LF-based theory. The proposal that he disagrees with is defining D-structure in terms of LF chains, a central assumption that carries over (in terms of D-sets) to the present approach. He seems to me to argue for the existence of D-structure and of derivations, but the proposal he criticizes in fact assumes that a D-structure exists and that a derivation links LF and D-structure. The points he raises are in part relevant, however, for the present theory, where no syntactic derivations are countenanced.

First, Chomsky notes the argument from the Head Movement Constraint for derivations. He points out that when a head X raises into another one Y, which subsequently raises further, we end up with a structure that given certain assumptions about indexing violates the HMC:

(21) $[Y_x \quad X_y \quad Y_x]$ ... t_x ... t_y ...

Although every step in the derivation obeyed the HMC, the resulting representation does not: there is a head between X_y and its trace t_y, namely t_x (see also Chomsky and Lasnik 1993).

"The point is that while the derivation from D-structure to S-structure meets the condition HMC step by step, its S-structure output violates the condition. We must somehow reconstruct the D- to S-structure derivation to determine whether the conditions of UG are satisfied" (Chomsky 1987, 195). But this appears to beg the question on two counts. First, the assumption that the S-structure output violates the condition is not necessary. Whether or not this is the case depends on the indexing structure of the intermediate trace. An indexing that avoids the HMC violation in (21) would be (22), as proposed in Baker 1988:

(22) $[Y_x \quad X_y \quad Y_x] \quad \ldots \quad t_{x,y} \quad \ldots \quad t_y$

The generalization that a category can have only one index would choose between (21) and (22), but this restriction is dubious on independent grounds. (Cf., e.g., Lasnik 1989; Sportiche 1983). Second, the assumption that an indexing along the lines of (22) is a reconstruction of the D- to S-structure derivation again begs the question: is the D- to S-structure derivation a reconstruction of the indexing/chain structure or vice versa? In chapter 5 I shall briefly return to this issue. The version of the copying theory of reconstruction developed there will entail that a head-trace/copy has all the relevant indices (as in (22)) to satisfy the HMC at LLF.

Chomsky also comments on the treatment of the ECP in Lasnik and Saito 1984 and Chomsky 1986b. "Within certain rather plausible theories, traces of movements must be deleted in the course of a derivation from D-structure to LF. If this is correct, then D-structure will not be reconstructible from LF (or, possibly, S-structure depending on exactly where the traces are deleted)" (Chomsky 1987, 195). But under my proposals (here and in earlier work) D-structure (or the D-set) contains only the root positions of chains, so it is unclear why deletion of intermediate traces should make D-structure unrecoverable. The present theory (but not the one criticized by Chomsky) is of course incompatible with a Lasnik-and-Saito–type multilevel solution to the ECP. (For alternative theories see Rizzi 1990; Manzini 1992a.)

Third, Chomsky notes that certain reflexive clitics can be associated only with D-structure subjects (see Rizzi 1986a), while others also accept derived subjects (Borer and Grodzinsky 1986). One possible explanation is that the first type of reflexive chooses its antecedent at D-structure but the second type at a derived level. Notice that this account would translate straightforwardly to the LLF theory: some reflexives must choose their antecedent from members of the D-set. Problems would arise, however, within the standard minimalist theory that dispenses completely with the type of concept apparently required here.

Chomsky contrasts the preceding explanation with Rizzi's proposal of a local binding condition for chains, which as he notes would be violated by the second type of reflexive clitic. But the question of whether there is a local binding condition on chain-links is distinct from the question of whether D-structures/sets are abstracted from chains. This remains true even if on the basis of Rizzi's argument the local binding condition was widely (though, as I argued in section 1.2, incorrectly) taken as evidence for a representational view. Suppose that the evidence from clitics against the local binding condition were accepted. It is quite consistent to reject the local binding condition but to maintain that D-structure/set is a function of chain-structure.

Finally, Chomsky also observes that "in actual linguistic work, one finds that the D- to S-structure mapping is almost invariably used, later to be translated into an S-structure algorithm of some sort." This is, of course, a correct description of actual practice, but the question is, precisely, is this practice correct? He continues with a remark with which I am naturally in full agreement: "It is often assumed that an S-structure algorithm is somehow preferable on general grounds to a D- to S-structure mapping, but it is difficult to attach much sense to this idea. The question appears to be at root empirical, though subtle" (Chomsky 1987, 195).

Riemsdijk (1987) joined this debate. He attributed the following general consideration to Chomsky 1987. Properties of chains that the corresponding movement rules do not have "never play a role in any syntactic principle. For example, no principle is sensitive to the number of links in the chain. This in itself is a good reason for being suspicious of chains" (Riemsdijk 1987, 20). But the reason why there are no syntactically relevant properties of chains that movement rules do not have is simply that under trace theory the concept of chain is weaker than that of Move α. If Move α is taken to be the set of tree-pairs that are its input and output, chains can correspond to the set of output trees only.

As for the example of counting the number of chain-links, note that movement has a corresponding property, the number of steps in a derivation. Whether in fact any principles refer to this number does not help to decide the issue: such a principle is stateable both representationally and derivationally. (Notice that a related but different consideration could be relevant. If there are both lowering rules and chain-link/derivational step counting principles, then these could give different predictions in cases where some element is raised into its own trace left by lowering. It seems, however, that step counting principles are unnecessary—if there are no lowering rules then the issue does not arise.)

Riemsdijk's depiction is in fact the reverse of the actual situation: as discussed earlier, there are multilevel properties of Move α that chains do not have, which appear to play no syntactic role. Thus no syntactic principle refers to the putative intermediate structures in a derivation (they are not ordered, and so forth).

Riemsdijk considers "split topicalization" constructions like (23); as he shows, they exhibit the usual movement diagnostics (chain diagnostics in our terms) but apparently have no well-formed source. In (23) there are two determiners associated with the head noun, which could not normally co-occur, as (24) shows:

(23) Einen Wagen hat er sich noch keinen leisten konnen
     a   car   has he refl yet   none   afford could
    'As for cars, he has not been able to afford one yet.'

(24) a. *einen keinen Wagen
    b. *keinen einen Wagen

Riemsdijk argues that a chain-theoretical analysis where the head of the chain would be the NP *einen Wagen* is problematic, since it would not predict that the gap must be always in the source position and that the ordering restrictions that hold in general between adjectives and between complements must be obeyed also by the split NP. (25) exemplifies this with adjectives:

(25) a.   Ein Amerikanisches Auto kann ich mir kein neues leisten
        an American   car can I   refl no   new   afford
        'As for an American car I cannot afford a new one.'
    b. *Ein neues Auto kann ich mir kein Amerikanisches leisten

(26) a.   ein neues Amerikanisches Auto
    b. *ein Amerikanisches neues Auto

He proposes instead that it is the N′ constituent that undergoes movement, leaving the determiner behind. The determiner in topic position is then the result of the (marked) processes of regeneration and relexicalization he postulates. Assuming that X′-theory holds at the post-movement stage, X′-movement can satisfy it provided that regeneration inserts the XP node dominating the moved element, and optionally the determiner node. The determiner *ein* can then be inserted by relexicalization, a process that can spell out "words that are fully determined by the features of the head of the moved phrase" (Riemsdijk 1987, 18). Riemsdijk presents the data as an argument for a derivational conception of syntax (with some qualifications). But the argument does not go through, since the analysis is compatible with both views. Thus a representational theory that adopts X′-chains could equally well be supplemented with the processes of regeneration and relexicalization. Riemsdijk appears to draw the same conclusion himself.

Recently, Chomsky (1994) has commented again on the idea of treating the HMC representationally, in terms rather similar to those of his earlier remarks. He considers the HMC case together with phenomena in segmental phonology where "such phenomena are pervasive." I shall pass over the phonological examples. Although in principle the same remarks might apply, their relevance to the issue of the syntactic mapping is unclear, given the assumption that the PF computation "modifies structures (including the internal structure of lexical entries) by processes sharply different from those that take place before entry into the PF component" (Chomsky 1994, 8).

"Typically," according to Chomsky, "derivation involves simple steps expressible in terms of natural relations and properties, with the context that makes them natural 'wiped out' by later steps of the derivation and not visible in the representations to which it converges" (Chomsky 1994, 6). But of course the question is precisely this; are they visible in those representations or not? As Chomsky notes, "In all such cases, it is possible to formulate the desired result in terms of outputs."

He takes the example of N incorporating to V, leaving the trace t_N, with the V + N complex raising to I, leaving the trace t_V. He then comments on treating the HMC "in terms of the (plausible) assumption that the trace is a copy" (see above and chapter 5 below); "[b]ut surely this is the wrong move." He considers the solution an "artifice." "The relevant chains at LF are (N, t_N) and (V, t_V), and in these the locality relation eliminated by successive raising is not represented. . . . These seem to be fundamental properties of language, which should be captured not obscured" (Chomsky 1994, 6).

The argument is reminiscent of early objections to trace theory. In "Who did John see" there is a local relation between the main verb and the object selected by it, which appears to be destroyed by Wh-movement. Surely, the objection went, it is an artifice to encode this local relation at S-structure, where it does not obtain any more, by means of a trace. At S-structure the relevant object category is the wh-phrase, which is not in a local relation here with the verb. But the objection is not valid, since we do not know a priori if a relevant local relation holds at the later level; this is an empirical issue. We do not know a priori what the relevant object category is at this level either: the wh-phrase, the trace, or some other entity perhaps composed of these—again, an empirical issue.

The empirical character of the problem does not change if the question is put differently: are traces (understood inclusively) or derivations, or perhaps both, needed? Is the syntactic computation "derivational or representational"? Here again "the questions are ... empirical, turning basically on explanatory adequacy" (Chomsky 1994, 5). Given independent evidence for traces, the issue of the locality of the verb-object relation no longer provides an empirical distinction between the two alternatives. Returning to head chains, here also we do not know a priori if "[t]he relevant chains at LF are (N, t_N) and (V, t_V)," or rather (N, N, N) and (V + N, V + N) under the copying theory, where the local relation is present at LF. Again, given independent evidence for the copy theory (cf. Chomsky 1992 and chapter 5 below), these local relations cannot be used as empirical grounds that distinguish the two approaches: both can account for the phenomena. There is no a priori reason why the fundamental property of syntactic computation must be the existence of local relations destroyed before the output stage (no copies, no traces) or the presence of these local relations in the output representations, whose existence here would only be "obscured" by a theory that attempted to capture them through postulating other "artificial" levels of representations.

There is some evidence for concepts that seem necessary in a representational theory of syntax, like traces, copies, and chains, and little evidence for the additional derivational apparatus. But the evidence based on the locality relations of the HMC appears to be neutral between derivational and representational approaches, just as the locality of subcategorization relations is neutral between theories with or without traces.

1.10   Appendix 2

Consider how syntactic structures are composed of lexical items in the monostratal radically minimalist framework. The correct answer may well be that the question belongs to the theory of performance: the competence theory of syntax only provides a set of conditions that the object assembled by some distinct component of the mind must meet. I will nevertheless sketch here a way of assembling syntactic representations that can in principle be part of competence theory under the radically minimalist hypothesis, a system that does not involve any intermediate representations.

Take a sentence like "Marie embrasse t Pierre," where t is the trace of the verb. The chain [embrasse,t] can be read off LLF; the position of the trace is in the D-set. But if (L)LF is projected from the lexicon, then we may want to know through which position the verb *embrasse* is to project its thematic and other projectional requirements *before* we have an LLF representation. Suppose, then, that the chain [embrasse,t] is formed before LLF is projected, that is, it is formed presyntactically.

What are the implications of presyntactic chain formation for lexical insertion? The first step in the assembly of a syntactic representation must still be the retrieval of a category from the lexicon. A lexical head L will project a structure that expresses its projectional requirements. L will either project directly, or if an (ordered) set of empty categories has been added to L, then in the position of the last empty category (the root of L's chain). Thus if the main verb in English remains in situ overtly, it will project its X'- and selectional structure in situ. In contrast, French main verbs form a chain with a trace and project their X'- and selectional requirements through this chain in the position of the trace.

Take the operation of Form Chain, which adds empty categories (or copies) to be unordered with respect to lexical projection. When it applies before projection, it creates head-chains; when it applies after, it builds XP-chains. If in the unmarked case no chains can be formed on intermediate projection levels, then this will be a consequence of projection applying in one block: it cannot be interspersed with chain formation.

In principle, there are two ways in which lexical insertion can then operate. It may either proceed cyclically, bottom to top, or in one step. Consider a phrasal category xP selected by y. Under the cyclic account xP is assembled first, so that it can satisfy the selectional requirement of y when y projects. Under the one-step procedure y and x project simultaneously, and we need to postulate a null placeholder element that satisfies the relevant selectional requirement of y. We may choose to think of this placeholder as a "position" to be filled by a matching category. Take, for example, the VP "saw the man." Under the cycle, the DP "the man" is assembled first, and this unit will be used on the VP-cycle to satisfy the relevant subcategorizational requirement of the verb. Under the one-step approach, the VP and the DP are constructed simultaneously, and therefore the DP cannot at this stage satisfy the verb's c-selectional feature. Hence it is necessary to postulate a placeholder entity for this purpose, to be replaced by the DP at some later stage, after this DP has been constructed.

Consider a structure like "$[_{IP} NP_X^* I [_{VP} e_x V NP]]$," the basic structure of an English sentence under the VP-internal subject hypothesis. I ignore the potential chain-relation between Infl and the verb and also the existence of DPs and the more articulate structure for the components of Infl for the purposes of this illustration.

(27) cyclic: a. project NP, NP*
           b. form chain [NP*,e]
           c. project VP (involves inserting "e" and NP)
           d. project IP (involves inserting VP)
           e. insert non-projected categories (NP* in IP)

(28) one-step: a. project NP, NP*, VP, IP (using empty placeholders
               ("positions") for selectional projection)
             b. form chain [NP*,e]
             c. insert all

The cyclic and the one-step derivations are sketched in (27) and (28), respectively. In the bottom-to-top cyclic approach, first the most deeply embedded NPs are constructed. Next the subject chain is formed, followed by the projection of the VP and insertion of the object and of the subject trace. Finally IP is projected and VP and the subject are inserted. In the one-step approach, all projection (here of subject, object, VP, and IP) takes place simultaneously. Projectional features are satisfied by placeholder positions. The subject chain is formed next (by adding an empty category to the maximal projection created), followed by insertion of all material, again a simultaneous procedure.

The cyclic approach is similar to the theory of derivation presented in Chomsky 1993. (The major difference between the cyclic system in (27) and the one in Chomsky 1993 is that in the latter Move α operates on syntactic substructures already formed. Thus step (27b) (as Move α) follows steps (27c) and (27d) in his approach.) Under the cyclic theory, intermediate syntactic structures must be generated. (This is so under both the Move α approach and the approach involving presyntactic chains.) For example, in a case like (27), at a certain stage in the derivation the VP would be formed that contains the object NP and the subject NP (under the Move α theory) or the trace of the subject NP (under the presyntactic chain theory). This is the stage where the operations in (27a–c), but not those in (27d–e), have been completed. The structure at this stage ("[$_{VP}$ NP V NP]" under the Move α theory and "[$_{VP}$ t V NP]" under the chain approach) is not the (L)LF representation of the full structure, nor can it be considered a lexical representation. Under the Move α theory it is not even a partial (L)LF representation in any straightforward sense: the subject is not in its LLF position.

Under the noncyclic, one-step theory of lexical insertion, no intermediate structures or partial LLF representations are generated. The phrasal projections of lexical elements are essentially lexical representations under this theory: they simply realize in a way that conforms to X'-theory some of the information present in the lexical entry of the head of the phrase. Similarly the chains can be thought of as abstract representations of lexical elements.

The assembly of an LLF representation will then consist of two steps: lexical projection (including chain construction, which may precede or follow it) and lexical insertion. The second step of LLF assembly is lexical insertion, which is instantaneous. All projections can be inserted simultaneously, creating no intermediate structures.

To take our concrete example again, look at the French "Marie embrasse Pierre." Assuming the VP-internal subject hypothesis and that V is in Infl, there will be at least two chains here: [V,e] and [Marie,e]. The empty category is added to V by Form Chain before V projects: V must then project through this empty category, given the Generalized Projection Principle. V-projection through the trace creates VP, I projects IP directly, and the Ns create NPs. Form Chain adds an empty category to the NP *Marie*. The selectional requirements of the verb at this stage must be satisfied by empty placeholders/positions. Next, all categories are inserted in one step. The Projection Principle is obeyed; it is the (root) trace of the subject argument that must satisfy the subject theta role of V, projected through the V-trace in VP.

Given this theory of one-step LLF assembly, if elements are chosen from the lexicon that do not fit together into a representation that is well-formed with respect to the syntactic projectional requirements, then no syntactic structure will be generated at all. (Recall that the Generalized Projection Principle is not a purely syntactic principle: some projectional requirements are syntactic, like categorial features and c-selection, and some semantic, like s-selection. Violating the semantic projectional requirements should not prevent generation of any syntactic structure.) This resolves the problem of overgeneration of intermediate structures. Note that we do not consider the X'-structures projected by lexical categories as proper syntactic structures, but simply as the normal form of the lexical input to syntax.

One might wonder if inappropriate choice of chain-structure should not be thought of as a residual overgeneration problem. If head chains are maximally two-membered, then this issue could only arise with XP-chains. Thus, suppose that some category is assigned a chain with more empty categories than the construction has positions to accommodate —say the subject *Marie* in our previous example, "Marie embrasse Pierre," is assigned a chain with more empty categories than there are spec positions for this chain to occupy. But on the assumption that chains, like the X'-projections of categories, are the abstract, syntactic input representation of the lexical elements, the matter reduces to the apparently ineliminable question of the proper lexical input. In the present framework it makes sense to consider even an XP-chain the (syntactic input) representation of the lexical category X that heads the XP: recall that the XP chain is formed independently of any other material in XP, and before any such material is inserted.

Chapter 2

Multiple Wh-/Neg-Relations and Subjacency

2.1 Introduction

Within the theory proposed here there are no movement derivations. The cluster of properties that in standard Principles and Parameters theory are taken to characterize Move α (ECP, Subjacency, MTC, reconstruction, Case-transmission) is captured by the concept of chains. Many of the Move α properties are stateable equally well as conditions on derivations or as conditions on representations. For example, as we have seen in chapter 1, the local binding condition on chains can be equivalent to prohibiting Move α against crossing over a coindexed category. Or to take another case, Rizzi's Relativized Minimality can equally well be thought of as a condition on representations restricting the set of categories that can legitimately intervene between members of a chain, or as a condition on movement that for particular instances of Move α states the set of uncrossable categories. This remains true also if we think of Relativized Minimality in terms of the derivational economy principle of the minimalist framework, that the length of the Move α steps should be minimized. As noted earlier, at least on this general level of discussion the restriction could equally well refer to the length of chain-links.

The Subjacency principle, however, has been argued to be a condition on the movement rule itself (Lasnik and Saito 1984, 1992). If true, this is problematic for a theory without movement. I shall argue first, in section 2.2, that it is neither necessary nor desirable to consider Subjacency as a constraint on Move α.

A related problem, but distinct from the question of the existence of constraints on derivations, has to do with a bifurcation of movement rules. Standard Principles and Parameters theory incorporates the assumption that only overt—that is, pre-S-Structure movement—is subject to Subjacency; LF movement is immune to its effects. This problem is independent of the question of whether Subjacency is a condition on derivations or on representations. Holding the former view, one would ask whether LF movement is constrained by Subjacency. Adopting the latter (the correct one, as I shall argue), the question is whether we need to require only S-structure but not LF chains to obey Subjacency.

Let us call wh-relations that cannot cross island boundaries (and are generally taken to show Subjacency effects) primary wh-relations. The remaining wh-relations, which can bridge islands (and are often thought of as not obeying Subjacency), are then the secondary ones. Primary wh-relations are generally taken to be expressed by overt movement, secondary ones by LF movement (cf., e.g., Watanabe 1991). In section 2.3 I argue (essentially following Longobardi 1991) against the claim that overt movement, but not LF movement, is constrained by Subjacency. The relevant distinction is different and cannot be treated in terms of pre- versus post-S-structure movement, but it can be straightforwardly expressed in a representational framework like the present one.

In section 2.4 I argue further that a theory incorporating any such bifurcation of the movement/chain dependencies with respect to Subjacency is conceptually and empirically problematic. This argument is relatively theory-neutral, pointing to the necessity of constraining both primary and secondary wh-relations by Subjacency in all current frameworks, including the radically minimalist approach.

In section 2.5 I discuss wh-relations in languages of the Chinese-Japanese type, proposing a pied-piping parameter that differentiates English from Japanese. In section 2.6 I discuss how Watanabe's account of Superiority facts in these two language-types can be integrated into the theory put forward here.

2.2   Subjacency: Derivation or Representation

Lasnik and Saito (1984, 1992) have provided three arguments for the claim that Subjacency must be stated on the rule of Move α itself rather than on output representations, as proposed for example by Freidin (1978)—a conclusion incompatible with a radical minimalist framework that has no rule of Move α.

Note, first, that a constraint on Move α is equivalent to a constraint stated on two levels of representation: the input and the output of the rule.

Very few constraints can even be suspected to necessitate such a two-level statement. Apart from Subjacency, only the Head Movement Constraint is a candidate (see chapter 5). Thus, a conceptually desirable, natural restriction is that no constraint can involve more than one level of representation. Such a restriction, of course, follows from the radical minimalist hypothesis that there are only (two) interface levels, each with its own constraints. A constraint on the rule of Move α is therefore clearly undesirable.

(A reviewer suggests that one could avoid this problem by viewing derivational conditions representationally as locality conditions on traces that must hold for *every* phrase marker in the derivation. However, the same problem would arise: there are very few constraints that might be thought of as necessitating such universal quantification over levels, so the natural restriction would be that no constraint can so quantify. Notice that anaphoric phenomena would not provide evidence for such universal quantification, since multiple-level accounts can easily be restated at (L)LF; cf. Barrs 1986 and chapter 5 below.)

Consider the evidence Lasnik and Saito provide. Their first argument has to do with the adjacency requirement in the *wanna*-type contraction phenomena. They assume Pesetsky's (1982) analysis, according to which such contraction requires strict adjacency; not even empty categories are allowed to intervene. Pesetsky's idea is that in structures like (1) the apparently intervening PRO element is in fact generated on the right side of I′ as in (1b):

(1) a. I wan+ PRO +na go there
   b. I wan+ [[+na go there] PRO]

Generating PRO on the right side is made possible by the assumption that the pre-I′ position of the English subject is made obligatory by the adjacency condition on Case-asignment. Since PRO requires no Case, no condition on Case-assignment can force it to precede I′.

Lasnik and Saito consider the case of adjunct extraction from the embedded clause as in (2).

(2) Why do you wan+ [t [+na go there t′]]

They point out that the assumption that the ECP requires an intermediate trace in the spec-CP of the embedded clause creates a problem for Pesetsky's minimal analysis of contraction. Given the presence of t in (2), the strict adjacency requirement between *want* and *to* is not satisfied.

Lasnik and Saito's solution to this problem is to assume that this trace is present only at the level of LF, where the ECP applies. (Irrelevantly for the present argument, they take the trace to be created by a lowering and raising application of Move α.) Thus at S-structure and at PF strict adjacency holds, and the minimal analysis of contraction can apply. It follows that Subjacency cannot be a condition on S-structure representations, since it would force the presence of the intermediate trace in spec-CP in examples like (2), preventing contraction. But (2) is a perfect case of contraction. (Note that one can restate for argument extraction the point that Subjacency as a condition on S-structure representations would incorrectly prevent contraction, if Subjacency is not taken to be relevant to adjunct chains.) Given the assumption that Subjacency does not constrain LF, the remaining possibility is to state it on the overt applications of the rule of Move α.

In Jaeggli's (1980) earlier analysis contraction is blocked by Case, but can apply across Caseless categories. This seems an equally minimal analysis, although Pesetsky's approach is arguably more natural. Thus, it is not clear that having to return to Jaeggli's analysis would be too high a price to pay for avoiding multilevel conditions. But it is not necessary to reject Pesetsky's elegant idea in order to preserve Subjacency as a condition on representations. As we shall see (sections 2.3, 2.4), the relations captured by LF movement in standard Principles and Parameters theory are constrained also by Subjacency. Thus the assumption that this constraint must hold at S-structure can be rejected, voiding the argument. At the level of LF the intermediate trace can be present and Subjacency satisfied even if no trace shows up at S-structure.

The argument is problematic even apart from conclusions to be reached shortly. The point Lasnik and Saito make depends on their analysis, highly idiosyncratic by now, of the clausal structure as COMP+S, with a single COMP position. Given the well-motivated CP structure nothing prevents extending Pesetsky's idea to the intermediate trace in spec-CP. Since this element needs no Case-assignment, it can freely occur on the right of CP, as in (3):

(3) Why do you wan+ [[+na go there t′] t]

Under the analysis in (3) we again have strict adjacency, and no conclusion follows with respect to Subjecency. As far as this data is concerned, Subjacency may hold at S-structure.

Lasnik and Saito's (1984) second argument for taking Subjacency as a condition on Move α involves adjacency of Case-assignment in ECM structures like (4):

(4) John believes her to like Mary

(5) Why does John believe [t [her to like Mary t']]

The structure of the argument is exactly the same: an apparent problem for Subjacency as condition on S-structure representations is created by the fact that the intermediate trace must not be present at this level to enable Case-assignment to operate under strict adjacency. The same problems arise: (*a*) Is strict adjacency really important to maintain? (*b*) Contrary to the standard view, Subjacency in fact holds at LF (see below). (*c*) Given the CP analysis of the clause, using Pesetsky's solution we can place the trace to the right of C'.

A third argument for Subjacency as a derivational condition is in Lasnik and Saito 1992, connected with the fact that an intervening *that* creates no ECP violation in the case of adjunct extraction:

(6) Why did John say that Mary fixed the bike t

They analyze (6) as involving successive cyclic movement, with a trace left in the intermediate "COMP" followed by S-structure insertion of *that*. In the LF component, *that* would delete and a trace would be created in its place to satisfy the ECP. Again, Subjacency cannot be a constraint on the S-structure representation they propose. At this level, (6) would violate the constraint, there being no intermediate trace. This account is quite complex: a trace is inserted, then deleted, and then inserted again. *That* is inserted and then deleted. In any case, except for (*a*), which is irrelevant to this data, the objections to the earlier two arguments apply here also.

In sum, there appears to be no reason to consider Subjacency to be a condition on Move α, and the radical minimalist hypothesis that Move α does not exist can be maintained.

2.3   Primary and Secondary Wh-Relations

Let us turn next to the question of whether secondary wh-relations, those standardly expressed by LF movement, obey Subjacency. On the basis of contrasts like the one between (7) and (8), it is generally assumed that this constraint is relevant only for overt movement.

(7) a. ??What did John wonder who bought t
    b. ??What did John deny the claim that Mary bought t
    c. ?*Who did John go there before Mary met t

(8) a.   Who wondered who bought what
          (relevant interpretation: "For which pair (x,y), x wondered who
          bought y")
    b.   Who denied the claim that Mary bought what
          (relevant interpretation: "For which pair (x,y), x denied the
          claim that Mary bought y")
    c.   Who went there before Mary met who
          (relevant interpretation: "For which pair (x,y), x went there
          before Mary met y")

The structures in (7) exhibit typical Subjacency violations. According to
the standard analysis, here overt wh-movement has created an antecedent
trace relation that crosses an island (wh-island in (7a), complex NP island
in (7b), adjunct island in (7c)). This results in mild-to-medium unacceptability, the hallmark of Subjacency.

    Still within the standard framework, the LF structures corresponding
to (8) on the interpretation indicated, are those in (9) (ignoring irrelevant
details):

(9) a. What, who wondered who bought t
    b. What, who denied the claim that Mary bought t
    c. Who, who went there before Mary met t

In (9), the wh-in-situ moved to the scopal position that is interpretively
appropriate for it. As is generally assumed since Huang 1982, the LF
movement accomplishing this appears not to be subject to Subjacency: the
violation of (7) is absent here.

    The same distinction could be captured within the radically minimalist
framework. In this theory, lexical material must be in the same position at
LF as it is at PF. Thus the LF structures of (8) will be those in (10), where
SM is the empty expletive functioning as a scope marker of the wh-in-situ:

(10) a. SM_x Who wondered who bought $what_x$
     b. SM_x Who denied the claim that Mary bought $what_x$
     c. SM_x Who went there before Mary met who_x

    Recall that the empty scope marker in these structures is an expletive
element, different from the contentive category that occurs in cases of

"overt operator movement" of the standard framework. Thus the difference between the two types of chains could be characterized by reference to whether the head of the chain is an expletive or a contentive element. This would recreate the distinction between the overt and LF movement.

Alternatively, we could distinguish primary and secondary wh-chains in the following way. There is a spec-head requirement imposed by a +WH C: its spec position must be filled by a wh-phrase. Primary wh-chains are headed by a wh-phrase that satisfies this condition. Other wh-chains are secondary. Thus in English all wh-phrases in SPEC-CP are heading primary wh-chains, and all wh-in-situ are in secondary wh-chains. The distinction between primary (Subjacency-observing) and secondary wh-relation would then correspond to the division between primary and secondary wh-chain. In other words, Subjacency could be stated as a constraint on primary chains only.

Longobardi (1991) provides clear evidence that with respect to Subjacency, the distinction between primary and secondary chains is empirically superior to the distinction between overt and LF movement. He shows that the scope rule for Italian negative phrases like *nessuno* respects Subjacency. These negative phrases are in situ at PF, but within standard Principles and Parameters theory have to raise at LF, since they show ECP-type effects (Kayne 1981; Rizzi 1982). The usual subject-object asymmetry shows up, for example, in (11), where *niente* but not *nessuno* can take wide scope.

(11) a. Non pretendo che nessuno dica questo
         not I-require that no one   says that
     b. Non pretendo che Gianni dica niente
         not I-require that Gianni says nothing

As Longobardi points out, (12a) and (13a) illustrate that the scope marker *non* can in principle be at an unbounded distance from the negative phrase so long as no complex NP boundary intervenes as in (12b) and (13b).

(12) a.   Non approverei che tu gli consentissi di vedere nessuno
           'I would not approve that you allow him to see anybody'
     b. *Non approverei la tua proposta di vedere nessuno
           'I would not approve of your proposal of seeing anybody'

(13) a.   Non credo che sia possible che ci consenta di fare niente
           'I do not believe that it is possible that he allows us to do
            anything'

b. *Non credo alla possibilita che ci consenta di fare niente
   'I do not believe the possibility that he allows us to do anything'

(14) and (15) show that CED effects are equally observed:

(14) a.   Non sara possibile chiamare nessuno
          'It will not be possible to call anyone'

   b.   (Sentential Subject Condition:)
        ?*Chiamare nessuno sara possible
        'To call no one will be possible'

(15)   (Adjunct Condition:)
   a.   *Non fa il suo dovere per aiutare nessuno
        'He does not do his duty in order to help anyone'
   b.   *Per ottenere nulla ha fatto il suo dovere
        'In order to obtain nothing has he done his duty'

Since within the standard framework these negative phrases do not overtly move to their scope positions, the fact that they obey Subjacency is a serious problem for the claim that only overt movement obeys this condition. Suppose, however, that we assume that negative phrases are related to their scope positions in order to satisfy some requirement imposed by the +NEG head (cf. e.g., Brody 1990b, Haegeman and Zanuttini 1991)—say a spec-head requirement of the neg-criterion that a +NEG head must have a neg-phrase spec. Just as in the case of wh-relations, we can now distinguish primary neg-relations from secondary ones. Primary neg-relations will be those that are necessary to satisfy the spec-head requirement of the "neg-criterion," and these are subject to Subjacency. This accounts for all the examples above. Secondary neg-relations, just like secondary wh-relations, can occur in Subjacency islands, as exemplified in (16), also from Longobardi:

(16) a.   (Sentential Subject Constraint:)
          (?)Chiamare nessuno [secondary neg-phrase] servira a niente,
          ormai
          'To call nobody will do any good now'
   b.   (Adjunct Condition:)
          Non fa niente per aiutare nessuno [secondary neg-phrase]
          'He does not do anything in order to help anyone'

Thus the distinction between primary and secondary neg-relations is more adequate empirically than that between overt and LF movement.

There is evidence from Japanese-type languages that the wh-relations divide in the same fashion. The situation is somewhat complicated by the possibility in these languages of "large scale pied-piping" (see, e.g., Nishigauchi 1990; Pesetsky 1987; Watanabe 1991). Pesetsky's *ittai*-test to show that wh-in-situ in these languages can be subject to Subjacency is controversial (Lasnik and Saito 1992), but Watanabe provides examples that exactly parallel Longobardi's neg-relation cases. Thus he points out that for those speakers that detect wh-island violations with a single wh-phrase, there is a contrast between (17a) and (17b):

(17) a.   John-wa [Mary-ga nani-o   katta   [ka-dooka]] dare-ni
          top   nom   what-acc bought whether   who-dat
          tazuneta no
          asked   Q
          'Who did John ask t whether Mary bought what'
    b. ??John-wa [Mary-ga nani-o   katta   [ka-dooka]] Tom-ni
          top   nom   what-acc bought whether   dat
          tazuneta no
          asked   Q
          'What did John ask Tom whether Mary bought t'

This is as expected, given Longobardi's data: in (17b) [nani-o,SM] forms a primary chain that violates Subjacency. In (17a) the same chain is secondary, the primary chain being [dare-ni,SM], and therefore allowed to cross an island. (Watanabe actually argues against an approach in terms of what I call primary and secondary chains, but in my view not very convincingly; cf. section 2.5.)

2.4 Secondary Chains are Parasitic

It is then possible to reproduce the LF/overt-movement distinction with respect to Subjacency in the radically minimalist theory, and such a reconstruction has important empirical advantages. But there are strong reasons for considering this at most an intermediate conclusion. I shall now argue that the generalization that secondary wh-chains (i.e., those whose presence is not necessary to satisfy the Wh-Criterion) do not obey Subjacency is in fact incorrect, being based on observations of a non-revealing subset of the relevant data. Thus the primary wh-relations (overt-movement type) and the secondary ones need not be distinguished for the purposes of stating Subjacency in any way—whether as movement

versus interpretation (Chomsky 1993), movement versus annotation (in
the spirit of Williams 1986), two types of movement (standard Principles
and Parameters theory) or two types of chains (above).

As has been noted, the assumption that only certain instances of Move
α obey Subjacency (either as a constraint on the rule or as a constraint on
the output representation/chain) is conceptually problematic, since there
is no obvious explanation of why overt Move α should differ in this way
from its LF counterpart. As we have seen, there are proposals that make
primary and secondary wh-relations maximally different by using two
different mechanisms to capture them. While such theories are perfectly
compatible with the nonderivational minimalist framework defended here,
they face the difficulty of accounting for the quite substantial similarities
between primary and secondary wh-relations, like those having to do with
the MTC and the ECP.

The other possible approach to the problem is to make primary and
secondary wh-relations as similar as possible. Thus Nishigauchi 1990 and
Pesetsky 1987 have argued, like Chomsky and Williams, that Subjacency
constrains all movement rules. But in contrast to the latter two authors,
Nishigauchi argued that (in my terms) both primary and secondary wh-
relations are movement relations and are thus constrained by Subjacency.
In a related proposal, Pesetsky claimed that all primary and a well-defined
subset of secondary wh-relations (involving wh-phrases that are not D-
linked) are to be captured by Move α and constrained by Subjacency.
These approaches have the advantage of not having to explain the un-
controversial similarities between primary and secondary wh-relations
—these are expected under a theory that expresses both relations using
the same concept. (There are problems with both Nishigauchi's and
Pesetsky's proposals; see Lasnik and Saito 1992.)

Elaborating and generalizing ideas in Longobardi 1991 and Kayne
1983, I shall argue that the general approach of Nishigauchi and Pesetsky
is correct: primary and secondary wh-relations should be expressed by the
same mechanism and despite appearances are subject to the same restrictions. At the same time I shall argue that the treatment of Subjacency
by all of these four proposals is empirically inadequate, since they fail to
capture the central locality property of the secondary wh-relations.

Let us turn to the facts that motivate the assumption that secondary
wh-relations are not subject to Subjacency. The examples indicating this
in (8) are reproduced here as (18):

(18) a. Who wondered who bought what?
          (relevant interpretation: "For which pair (x,y), x wondered who
          bought y")
      b. Who denied the claim that Mary bought what
          (relevant interpretation: "For which pair (x,y), x denied the claim
          that Mary bought y")
      c. Who went there before Mary met who
          (relevant interpretation: "For which pair (x,y), x went there
          before Mary met y")

Kayne (1983) points out a certain similarity between parasitic gap constructions and multiple-wh-structures in relation to a specific licensing
effect. Given a wh-in-situ in a construction where it violates Superiority,
for instance (19a), another wh-phrase under the appropriate structural
conditions can "license" it, remedying the violation (cf. (19b)):

(19) a. *I'd like to know where who hid it
      b. ?I'd like to know where who hid what
      c. *I'd like to know where who said (that) what was hid

(20) a.   a man that anyone who talks to e admires t
      b. *a man that anyone who talks to e realizes (that) t is brilliant

   Kayne claims that the licensing of one wh-phrase by another in (19) is
under the same generalization as the licensing in a parasitic gap construction. He argues that licensing of the parasitic gap in (20) by the chain
of a primary gap takes place under the same structural conditions under
which a wh-phrase can license another one that violates Superiority. Thus
as (19c) and (20b) exemplify, in a configuration in which a primary gap
could not license a parasitic one, a third wh-phrase cannot license a
wh-in-situ either. ((19c) and (20b) are not an exact minimal pair. This is
because a wh-in-situ can c-command another, while a parasitic gap generally must not c-command the primary gap—for independent reasons
that are irrelevant here; cf. Kayne 1983 and also chapter 3 below.)
   The licensing procedure operates quite generally with parasitic gaps.
That is, any parasitic gap that satisfies the appropriate structural conditions can be licensed by the chain of the real gap. Clearly if Kayne is
right and the phenomenon in (19) is accomplished by the same kind of
licensing, then wh-licensing should operate just as generally. It would be
quite curious to restrict licensing of wh-in-situ to those cases where this
wh-phrase violates some condition like Superiority.

But this observation already solves the Subjacency problem for secondary wh-relations. Just as a parasitic gap can occur inside an island because it is licensed by a primary chain, we expect secondary wh-relations to occur inside islands if they are invariably parasitic on other wh-relations.

Kayne made the important discovery that although parasitic gaps can occur inside islands, they are still sensitive to further island constraints inside the highest island domain containing them (see also Chomsky 1986b for relevant discussion). Thus we now expect that island effects will show up also with a wh-in-situ if it is separated from its licensing chain by two islands. If we restrict our attention to the absorbed, "list" reading, then this prediction appears to be confirmed:

(21) (adjunct island inside a complex NP)
   a. Who was against proposals to leave without waiting for who
      (not: 'Which pair (x,y) x was against proposals to leave without waiting for y')

compare:
   b. Who wanted to propose to leave without waiting for who
      ('Which pair (x,y) x wanted to propose to leave without waiting for y')
   c. Who made the decision to leave without telling whom
      (not: 'Which pair (x,y) x made a decision to leave without telling y')

compare:
   d. Who decided to leave without telling whom
      ('Which pair (x,y) x decided to leave without telling y')

(22) (complex NP inside an adjunct island)
   a. Who left without denying the fact that Mary met whom
      (not: 'Which pair (x,y) x left without denying the fact that Mary met y')

compare:
   b. Who left without denying that Mary wanted to meet whom
      ('Which pair (x,y) x left without denying that Mary wanted to meet y')

(23) (complex NP inside another)
   a. Who was against proposals to find a topic to discuss with whom
      (not: 'Which pair (x,y) x was against proposals to find a topic to discuss with y')

compare:

b. Who was against proposals to tell Mary to try to discuss this with whom
   ('Which pair (x,y) x was against proposals to tell Mary to try to discuss this with y')

Although judgements are quite delicate, especially in the double complex-NP island case (23), nevertheless they seem to go as predicted, the examples involving multiple islands being worse under the relevant reading. I conclude that both primary and secondary (parasitic) wh-relations are constrained by Subjacency, and thus chains are uniform in obeying this constraint along with the MTC and the ECP.

Although he avoided discussing wh-relations, Longobardi (1991) has argued that LF (neg-) movement can be parasitic on some primary (neg-) chain. As he points out, his results provide strong evidence for the approach that takes Subjacency to be relevant for all movement/chain relations.

As noted in section 2.3, Longobardi showed that the relation of the Italian *nessuno*-type negative phrases to their scopal position, which in the standard framework is expressed by LF movement, is constrained by Subjacency. He also exemplified in detail the existence of (in our terms) secondary, parasitic neg-relations. The behavior of these is exactly parallel to that of parasitic wh-relations. As we have already seen, Longobardi showed that the primary neg-phrase can be separated from the parasitic one by an island boundary, as in (16), reproduced as (24):

(24) a.   (Sentential Subject Constraint:)
          (?)Chiamare nessuno [secondary neg-phrase] servira a niente, ormai
          'To call nobody will do any good now'
     b.   (Adjunct Condition:)
          Non fa niente per aiutare nessuno [secondary neg-phrase]
          'He does not do anything in order to help anyone'

But just as in the case of wh-in-situ, there can be only one island boundary between them. Some of Longobardi's evidence is in (25) and (26), where the secondary neg-phrase is separated by two island boundaries from the primary neg-phrase, resulting in ungrammaticality:

(25)   (Adjunct island inside Subject island:)
       *Partire per incontrare nessuno [secondary neg-phrase] servira a niente
       'To leave in order to meet no one will do any good'

(26)   (Adjunct island inside another:)
       *Non fa niente per scoprire la verita indagando su nessuno
       [secondary neg-phrase]
       He doesn't do anything in order to discover the truth by
       investigating anyone'

Longobardi's results immediately generalize to wh-relations. In sum, not only the MTC and the ECP but also Subjacency are general conditions on all neg- and wh-relations. The assumption of the standard Principles and Parameters theory that Subjacency constrains overt but not LF movement is incorrect: there are relations that must be treated as LF movement in the standard framework but that still show Subjacency effects. An improved approach, in terms of primary and parasitic wh- and neg-relations, can correctly distinguish relations that cannot cross any islands from those that are able to cross one of the boundaries Subjacency imposes. Such a theory is already compatible with the LLF framework, but apparently still in need of further revision. On closer examination, it turns out to be necessary to extend Subjacency to both types of relations. Secondary wh- and neg-relations can cross an island because they are parasitic and not because they do not obey Subjacency. As evidence, just like ordinary parasitic gaps they can only cross a single island; inside this island they obey Subjacency. I shall not attempt here to choose among the many competing theories that account for the locality behavior of parasitic constructions (e.g., Kayne 1983; Chomsky 1986b; Frampton 1990). All of these are readily extendable to cover the general pattern of parasitic neg- and wh-structures. (For a promising recent theory essentially in the "connectedness" spirit, see Manzini 1992a and 1993.)

As Longobardi notes, neg-phrases do not seem to obey the nonsentential part of the subject, adjunct, and (complex) NP island conditions. Thus (27a), for example, where the neg-phrase is inside a nonsentential subject contrasts with (27b), the sentential subject case. Similarly, (28a), where the neg-phrase is in a nonsentential relative, is grammmatical, but (28b), with a sentential relative clause, is not:

(27) a. (?)La presenza di nessuno lo spaventerebbe
          'The presence of no one would frighten him'
      b. *Che fosse presente nessuno lo spaventerebbe
          'For no one to be present would frighten him'

(28) a.   Non abbiamo trovato [gli indici relativi a nessuno degli imputati in questione
'We have not found the clues relative to any of the defendants in question'

     b.   *Non cercavo una ragazza che fosse amica di nessuno
'I did not look for a girl who was friend with anybody'

Longobardi provides independent evidence for a percolation/pied-piping mechanism that will turn the whole (nonsentential) island containing a quantifier in such cases into a QP, here a neg-phrase. The situation is again similar in English multiple wh-constructions. Thus Fiengo et al. (1988) cite the following example to show that LF-movement of wh-in-situ can bridge two islands:

(29) Who remembers where pictures of who are on sale

But if the whole subject "pictures of who" is taken to be the wh-phrase, then the construction behaves in accordance with the earlier generalization: the parasitic wh-relation involving this wh-in-situ is separated from the primary one by exactly one island boundary.

Fiengo et al. (1988) argue against the assumption that wh-raising (in our terms the secondary wh-chain) affects the whole subject. Citing Huang (1982), they point out the contrast between (30a,b) and (30c,d):

(30) a.   What did people from where buy t
     b.   Who did pictures of who please t
     c.   *What did who buy t
     d.   *Who did what please t

If the whole subject was the wh-phrase in (30a,b), the structures would be on a par with those in (30c,d) and we would expect them to violate Superiority.

The argument is inconclusive, however. There is no need to take the pied-piping option in (30a,b), since the parasitic wh-in-situ is separated from the primary chain only by one island boundary. Pied piping *is* necessary in (29), but here it is also possible. As Lasnik and Saito (1992) note, an example like (31) "is dramatically improved on the reading where *who*$_3$ takes matrix scope, that is, where [(31)] is a matrix double question on *who*$_1$ and *who*$_3$" (Lasnik and Saito 1992, 119). Thus Superiority phenomena provoke no objection against taking the subject NP in (29) as the secondary wh-in-situ.

(31) Who$_1$ t$_1$ wonders what$_2$ who$_3$ bought t$_2$

(Fiengo et al. (1988) give another example, (32a), of a wh-in-situ inside two islands, but this is less easy to evaluate:

(32) a. Who remembers where we bought books that criticize who
     b. Who remembers where we told Mary that she shouldn't criticize what

It is not clear to what extent the embedded wh-object can be given an absorbed matrix scope interpretation in (32a). It is not clear if the example is indeed worse on such a reading than the equally complex (32b), where the wh-in-situ is embedded only in one island. The contrast is weaker than in (21) and (22), perhaps on a par with the one in (23). The weakening of the contrast in the NP-island cases could plausibly be attributed to the marginal possibility of "large-scale pied piping," discussed further in section 2.5.)

Consider why the postulated pied-piping mechanism does not show up fully on wh-phrases in primary, overt interrogative wh-chains:

(33) a. ?I wonder to whom Mary talked
     b. *I wonder [pictures of whom] Mary saw
     c. I wonder [whose mother] Mary talked to

Notice first of all that relative wh-phrases generally behave as predicted by the percolation mechanism postulated above: pied piping is possible so long as it does not cross sentential boundaries:

(34) a. the man [pictures of whom] Mary saw
     b. the man [near whom] Mary sat
     c. the man [whose mother] Mary talked to
     d. *the man [the pictures that showed who] Mary saw
     e. *the man [that John saw who] Mary said

This suggests that the ungrammaticality of (33b) and the marginality of (33a) is due to the impossibility not of Q-percolation, but rather of having a category that is a wh-phrase by percolation in the spec of a +WH CP. In terms of the standard minimalist theory, we can assume that this is because a percolated wh-feature cannot check the strong +WH feature of the C node. (In terms of the theory to be developed in chapter 4, the +WH C can be taken not to licence such a percolated wh-phrase in its spec.) Thus, contrary to what Fiengo et al. suggest, the lack of full parallel between percolation involved in overt Wh-movement (primary chains) and covert movement (secondary chains) does not necessarily show that "[t]he LF pied piping hypothesis must assume that LF pied piping of a [+wh] phrase into COMP is radically different [from] syntactic pied piping" (Fiengo et al. 1988, 87). (This criticism is well taken against the assumption that potentially unrestricted pied piping in English feeds the construction of covert Wh-movement/secondary chains, as such pied piping does not show up overtly anywhere. See Watanabe (1991) for a critique of some of Fiengo et al.'s (1988) remaining arguments against the syntactic pied-piping approach. I do not address here the question of elliptical answers, discussed in Nishigauchi 1990, Fiengo et al., (1988) and Lasnik and Saito 1992, among others, since no reasons have been given in the literature to think that this data contains potential evidence against pied piping. The worst-case scenario is that this test for pied piping is useless.)

The solution offered by Fiengo et al. (1988) to explain why wh-in-situ (and quantifiers generally) may occur in Subjacency islands runs as follows. First they adopt a variant of the Q-percolation approach but with important differences. They assume that "certain constructions properly containing QNPs may be construed as QNPs themselves that are subject to QR" (Fiengo et al. 1988, 93). Thus the island constituent containing a wh-phrase can be taken as a quantified phrase, making it subject to QR. QR once applied, the island becomes an A'-binder and therefore ceases to be a barrier, a point for which they provide independent evidence. The wh-in-situ can then raise out of the island and an apparent violation of Subjacency results.

This account, however, is designed to explain that wh-in-situ can in principle occur embedded in any number of island boundaries. If this is in general untrue, as I have argued, then clearly the account cannot be maintained. The mechanism provided would create no contrast between the examples in (21)–(23). Extended to neg-phrases, the contrast between (24) on one hand and (25) and (26) on the other should be nonexistent. Take (21)–(23): given the account in Fiengo et al., we cannot explain the lack of the absorbed, list-reading interpretation in the multiple-island cases. Their account allows, first, the higher island to QR to an A'-position, turning it into a non-island; then QR applies to the more deeply embedded island. This in turn neutralizes the lower island boundary, allowing the wh-phrase finally to move to the matrix CP. Thus this solution does not account for the contrasts between the *a* and *b* examples in (21)–(23), or the similar and clearer contrasts in the cases involving

neg-phrases, (24) versus (25) and (26). It will also not explain the contrast
between the acceptable absorbed multiple-island-internal wh-phrase in
(29) and the unabsorbable wh-in-situ in, for example, (22a).

2.5 Pied-Piping Parameters

Let us turn to wh-relations in Japanese-type languages. In these languages, wh-phrases surface in situ. As we have seen in the last section, all
wh- and neg-chains are constrained by Subjacency. Whether such a chain
shows these effects directly or only within the single island that it is
allowed to cross depends not on whether the wh- or neg-phrase is in situ
but rather on whether it is part of a primary or a secondary (parasitic)
chain.

But in-situ wh-phrases of primary wh-relations in Japanese can occur
within islands, indeed even within multiple islands, as exemplified by the
following sentences (from Watanabe 1991):

(35) a. John-wa [nani-o   katta   hito]-o   sagasite iru no?
        Top   what-acc bought person-acc looking for Q
        'What is John looking for the person who bought?'
     b. John-wa [[[[dare-o   hihansita] ronbun]-ga notta
        Top   who-acc criticized article-nom appeared
        zassi]-o   sagasite iru no
        journal-acc looking for Q
        'John is looking for the journal where an article that criticized
        who appeared'
     c. John wa [nani-o_x katta hito]-o sagasite iru no SM_x

The minimal hypothesis is that in-situ wh-phrases are related to their
scope positions in the same way in Japanese as in English. Thus within the
LLF theory we assume that Japanese also has an empty expletive scope
marker in the appropriate position associated through a chain with the
in-situ wh-phrase. But (35a) will then apparently have a representation
like (35c), the chain [nani-o_x,SM_x] violating Subjacency.

A number of authors, including Choe (1987), Nishigauchi (1990), and
Pesetsky (1987) have argued that this is possible not because Subjacency
does not constrain the wh-relation between *nani-o* and its scope position,
but rather because "large-scale pied piping" is an option. Watanabe 1991
contains a recent defense of this idea. These authors have proposed that in
a sentence like (35a), the wh-feature can percolate from the wh-word fur-

ther than usual, making the whole complex NP "nani-o katta hito-o" the wh-phrase that is associated with the relevant scope position. In (35b), percolation could continue up to the more inclusive complex NP. In present terms the correct structure for (35a) is then not (35c), but (36), where the scope marker is associated with the more inclusive wh-phrase:

(36) John wa [nani-o katta hito]-o$_x$ sagasite iru no SM$_x$

Thus the view is taken here that languages differ in their ability to percolate a wh- or more generally $[+Q]$ feature to some more inclusive node. Looking at percolation to NP nodes and adjuncts, Japanese is the most permissive: here any wh-phrase containing NP/adjunct can be considered $[+wh]$. As noted earlier (cf. (27) and (28) above), Longobardi (1991) shows that in Italian percolation of $[+Q]$ (including $[+wh]$ and $[+neg]$) is restricted not to cross sentential categories. In connection with Fiengo et al.'s example where a parasitic wh-chain appeared to cross two islands, I suggested that English also has the Italian degree of freedom with respect to percolation of $[+Q]$. The assumption that there is interlanguage variation here is natural, since syntactic pied piping also shows such variation even internally to English, being much freer in appositive relatives than in interrogatives, for example. Furthermore, the setting of the English/Italian ($-$sentential) versus Chinese/Japanese ($+$sentential) value of the parameter is plausibly related to the fact that inflection is independently known to have different properties in these two language-classes. For example, it could be assumed that the Chinese/Japanese type of inflection (as opposed to the English/Italian type) has the property that its maximal projection is not a barrier to $[+Q]$ percolation.

Consider using large-scale pied piping as a general explanation of the fact that in English multiple questions, the wh-in-situ can occur in islands. Using this mechanism with the Japanese degree of freedom one could also take all movement to be constrained by Subjacency. Under this approach, for example, in (37) the whole complex NP "the man that bought what" would be the relevant in-situ wh-phrase.

(37)   Who met the man that bought what

(38)   *the present [the man that bought which] you meet t

As noted in the previous section, a problem for such an approach is the fact, exemplified in (38), that overt wh-chains in English do not exhibit large-scale pied piping across sentential complements. (Cf. Fiengo et al. (1988) and Lasnik and Saito (1992) for this argument against

Nishigauchi's proposals.) The problem does not arise given the use of less radical pied piping for English proposed here. Nonsentential NPs and adjuncts can also pied pipe overtly in this language, as in (34) above.

Without an explanation of why overt and LF pied piping should differ in this way, it is not clear that anything would be gained by a large-scale pied piping analysis of English wh-in-situ. Such as analysis appears to exchange the puzzle of why Subjacency is restricted to overt movement for the puzzle of why large-scale pied piping is restricted to wh-phrases moved at LF. Lasnik and Saito take this to be an argument against large-scale pied piping in general, hence also against using this mechanism for Japanese. But given the evidence in section 2.4, this more general objection does not seem valid. There is no distinction between overt and LF movement with respect to pied piping, but rather a parameter set differently for English and Japanese.

Furthermore, as we have also seen in the previous section, English in-situ wh-phrases can be separated from their scope positions by at most one island. Inside this island, Subjacency appears to be fully observed by the in-situ wh-phrase, just as by other parasitic constructions, be they empty gaps or parasitic neg-phrases in Italian. This fact creates an even more serious difficulty for the proposal of treating English wh-in-situ in terms of Japanese-style large-scale pied piping, since under such a theory we expect structures like (22a), reproduced here as (39), to have the absorbed interpretation.

(39) Who left without denying the fact that Mary met whom

It should not matter how many island boundaries intervene between the in-situ wh-phrase and the chain of the wh-phrase in the relevant scope position. There is no reason why large-scale pied piping could not percolate a wh-feature high enough to make the largest complex NP the wh-phrase. Thus even though Nishigauchi's large-scale pied piping approach claims that Subjacency constrains all wh-relations, it does not seem capable of predicting that apart from the usual exception due to the parasitic nature of secondary English wh-relations, these relations generally show Subjacency effects.

The proposal defended here takes an intermediate position with respect to wh-feature percolation in English multiple wh-constructions. I claim that such pied piping by wh-in-situ is not as "large scale" as in Japanese but not nonexistent, either, as is generally assumed. The position that large-scale pied piping takes place in Japanese wh-relations but no pied piping at all in English secondary wh-relations has recently been defended in Watanabe 1991, as one aspect of his theory of empty operators. In the remainder of this section I shall compare his approach to the theory advanced here.

In Watanabe's theory, as in the present one, in Japanese primary wh-relations an empty operator associated with the wh-in-situ occurs under the relevant CP. In contrast to the theory of empty scope markers proposed here, he takes this operator to originate in the spec-DP position of the in-situ wh-phrase. The operator then moves to spec-CP in overt syntax. Based on these assumptions, he claims, first, that only overt movement is subject to Subjacency, and second, that the (apparent) lack of overt wh-movement and the option of large-scale pied piping is controlled by the same parameter: essentially, the option of allowing the empty operator to occur separately from the wh-headed NP.

The S-structure spec head requirement of a +WH C can thus be satisfied by the empty operator in Japanese, but not in English, where such an empty operator is either nonexistent or inseparable from the DP in which it occurs. Hence Japanese, but not English, can appear not to have overt movement. As for large-scale pied piping, the existence of this option in Japanese is attributed to the same parameter: the empty operator can be generated separately, as the spec of a category higher than the DP most immediately dominating the wh-word. Watanabe assumes that generating the wh-operator in its spec position will turn a DP into a wh-phrase.

Finally, Watanabe attempts to bring one further difference between English and Japanese under the same parameter. The indeterminate and quantificational elements are morphologically distinct in Japanese quantifiers but, he assumes, are fused in their English equivalents. He takes this to indicate that the syntactic relation between the two elements is also closer in English: the Q head of the QP complement of D raises to D in that language, but not in Japanese. He proposes that the "closeness" of this head-head relation correlates with the requirement of "closeness" between the empty operator to the relevant wh-head.

There are a number of problems with these proposals. First of all, Watanabe's zero-pied-piping account of English wh-in-situ, just like Nishigauchi's large-scale pied piping solution, cannot account for the data in the previous section. It cannot differentiate wh-in-situ in single islands from those in multiple (sentential) islands. Second, the suggested parameter appears untenable given Longobardi's Italian data. The morphologically fused nature of quantifiers that Italian exhibits does not seem to correlate with the necessity of overt movement (to satisfy the neg-criterion), since the latter is not shown by Italian neg-phrases. The inverse counterexample is furnished by Hungarian: here quantifiers are morphologically complex, essentially as in Japanese, but overt movement in primary wh-relations is obligatory.

If we exclude this correlation, the residue of Watanabe's parameter is still interesting: lack of large-scale pied piping correlates with the necessity of overt movement in primary wh-relations; according to him both are reflexes of the possibility of separating the null operator from the associated wh-head. But again, given the evidence that primary wh- and neg-relations fall under the same generalizations and thus should be treated in a parallel fashion, Italian appears to falsify the parameter. As Longobardi's data show, overt neg-movement is not forced in this language, but large-scale pied piping is not an option. If Italian had large-scale pied piping, we would expect neither primary nor parasitic neg-relations to show Subjacency effects.

Watanabe's proposal of relating the null operator to the spec-DP position of the wh-phrase also has a number of technical problems. First he needs to assume that there are two distinct mechanisms of wh pied piping: a category containing a wh-word can become a wh-phrase either by inheriting this feature through the standard feature percolation process from the wh-word, or in consequence of its spec being filled by an empty operator of the appropriate kind. The feature-percolation mechanism has to be retained, since by hypothesis the operator-driven wh-phrase creation is inoperative in English. Overt pied piping is manifestly possible, however.

As Watanabe notes, his proposal that the spec-DP position of the wh-in-situ in Japanese contains an empty operator, and that this is the element that overtly moves to spec-CP, also creates the problem of how the ECP is satisfied when the wh-phrase is an island, say an adjunct. Movement of the null operator then crosses this island in apparent violation of the ECP. Since the spec-DP operator is clearly not a referential argument, given a Lasnik-and-Saito/Barriers framework, it is necessary to delete some intermediate trace T_i that licenses (gamma-marks) the trace T_n of the operator in spec-DP position. Real ECP effects are then attributed to subsequent LF raising of the full DP. Such raising would be problematic in any minimalist framework, since in-situ wh-phrases behave consistently in a way that shows that they remain in situ at LF. Whether these include an anaphor, a bound pronominal, or a proper name, their construals all appear to show that no raising of the full DP takes place (see chapter 5).

Yet another problem has to do with Subjacency: why does movement of the empty operator out of an adjunct wh-phrase not violate this principle? Watanabe assumes that adjunction to adjuncts is not generally possible since it would interfere with theta role assignment (by the adjunct). He suggests that the adjunct island condition can be circumvented, however, through adjunction to the adjunct, when the adjunct is raised at LF to become an operator. But it is rather unclear why theta role assignment by a nonoperator adjunct is interfered with by adjunction to it, but theta role assignment (at LF) by the trace of the operator adjunct is immune to interference by adjunction to its antecedent. Furthermore, the assumption that the in-situ wh-adjunct raises at LF would again be problematic in a minimalist theory, where binding conditions must hold at LF.

(In fact Watanabe assumes, citing Pesetsky, that adjunction to operators is not allowed in general. An example like (40) must still be ruled out.

(40) *Who$_x$ did you wonder [which person that you talked to about t$_x$] I should invite

Watanabe's suggestion is that adjunction to an operator should be allowed if the adjoined element and the operator "form a unit at LF" as in the grammatical Japanese adjunct wh-in-situ case but not in (40). Technically this solves the problem, but it abolishes the theory of generally allowed adjunction to operators in favor of a stipulation for the case at hand. Note that adjunction to predicates/VPs is not similarly restricted.)

None of the above problems (the necessity of two pied-piping mechanisms, the unexpected behavior of the empty operator with respect to the ECP, and Subjacency) arises in the theory put forward here. According to this theory, an empty scope marker forms a chain with the in-situ wh-/neg-phrase, and primary and secondary wh-/neg-relations are distinguished in terms of whether the relation is necessary to satisfy the wh-/neg-criterion.

Watanabe in fact argues against such a theory. He makes the curious claim that the "null hypothesis is that Subjacency constrains only the mapping from D-structure to S-structure" (Watanabe 1991, 48). He

arguos for the approach that distinguishes primary and secondary
wh-relations in terms of overt and LF movement in the following way.
First he shows that certain relations like comparative deletion and scrambling must be treated in terms of S-structure movement in standard Principles and Parameters theory, since they show Subjacency effects and
license parasitic gaps. Next he observes that these relations are sensitive
to the presence of primary wh-chains. For example, comparative deletion
is blocked in (41).

(41) *[Minna-ga   [naze Paul-ga e yonda ka] siritagatteiru
      everyone-nom why   nom read Q know-want
      yori(mo)] John-ga   takusan-no hon-o   yonda
      than   nom many-gen book-acc read
      'John read more books than everybody wants to know why Paul
      read.'

This can be accounted for within the standard framework if an intervening spec-CP position associated with the wh-phrase that ultimately
creates the blocking effect is filled already at S-structure. Watanabe presents this type of evidence as an argument against taking the relevant
distinction to be between (in my terms) primary and secondary chains.
But the conclusion does not follow. The evidence demonstrates only that
within standard Principles and Parameters theory the spec-CP position
involved in a primary chain must be filled already by S-structure. This
position could be filled by a scope marker, without any movement having
taken place. Within the radically minimalist theory of wh-chains, the ungrammaticality of (41) and other similar cases is expected. Within this
theory an empty scope marker associated with the wh-phrase in situ fills
the relevant CP-spec position at LLF, creating a blocking effect for Subjacency.
   In fact, as we shall see in the next section, the spec position of the
+WH CP in Japanese probably contains an element that creates the
blocking effect for Subjacency and that is distinct from the scope marker
associated with the wh-phrase. Although I have been arguing against
Watanabe's claim that in Japanese the empty operator in spec-(+WH-)
CP starts out in spec-DP position (or in my terms forms a chain with that
position), this does not deny the presence of a category in spec-CP distinct
from the scope marker associated with the full wh-phrase. Watanabe's
analysis of Superiority and "Anti-superiority" in Japanese provides evidence for such an element.

2.6 Superiority and Anti-Superiority

As noted earlier, Watanabe assumes that the wh-associate (i.e., the remnant of the wh-phrase left behind after the null operator moves from spec-DP) moves at LF to join the null operator. Similarly, he takes wh-phrases of secondary wh-relations to move at LF to adjoin to the appropriate spec-CP. The main motivation for these assumptions is provided by his analysis of Superiority phenomena.

Watanabe proposes a novel version of the path-theoretical analysis (cf. Pesetsky 1982; Saito 1989; May 1985): he suggests that the wh-phrases must be in the same hierarchic command relation in the CP domain at LF as they or their traces are IP-internally at S-structure. This is intended as a subcase of a general principle of relation preservation:

(42) "A relation established at a certain point in the derivation must be maintained throughout" (Watanabe 1991, 101).

(Watanabe actually requires only that there be at least a single pair of wh-phrases in any CP satisfying (42), for reasons that need not concern us here.) He defines the notion of *seg(ment)*-command, which he takes to be the relevant relation for the condition in (42) (Chomsky's (1993) notion of *domain* appears to be a slight generalization of this). Seg-command is to be understood on the pattern of c- and m-command: the first segment dominating the category x must dominate the category y—with the crucial proviso that a category is not taken to be dominated by its own segment. It follows from this that x does not seg-command y if x is adjoined to y. (cf. the parallel requirement in Chomsky's definition of "domain": y is not in the domain of x if y contains x).

The crucial relations are exemplified in (43), where z and y are adjoined to x.

(43)

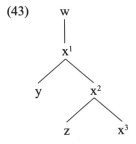

Here x seg-commands both y and z (first segment dominating x is w, w dominates y and z) and y seg-commands z (first segment dominating y is x^1, x^1 dominates z), but neither y nor z seg-commands x (the first segment dominating each, x^1 and x^2 respectively, does not dominate the category x, of which it is a segment (or in Chomsky's terms x contains y and z, so they are not in the domain of x). Of course z does not seg-command y (since x^2 does not dominate y).

Using the notation {X < Y} to express a relation where X seg-commands Y, consider the seg-command relations in the Superiority-violating structure (44b) and its grammatical counterpart (44a):

(44) a.   Who did you persuade t to give what to Bill
     b. *?What did you persuade who to give t to Bill

Looking first at IP-internal, S-structure seg-command relations between the in-situ wh-phrases, and the traces of the moved wh-phrases, we have {who < what} in both (44a) and (44b). Adjunction to spec-CP results in the LF CP-structures in (45):

(45) a.   b.

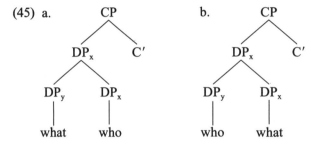

Consider the seg-command relations in (45). In (45a) *who* seg-commands *what*: the first segment (CP) that dominates the (two-segment) category of *who* dominates *what*. On the other hand, *what* does not seg-command *who*: the first segment that dominates *what* is the higher segment of DP_x, and a category is not dominated by its own segment. Thus the command relation at LF is the same as at S-structure, namely {who < what}. In (44b) the command relation IP-internally at S-structure is again {who < what}, but in (45b), at LF, it is {what < who}, for the same reasons as in the previous case. Thus the relation preservation principle (42) is violated.

The advantage of this analysis is that it can extend to the Japanese Anti-superiority phenomenon exemplified in (46):

(46) a. *Naze nani-o   John-ga   katta-no
        why what-acc   nom bought Q
        'What did John buy why'
     b. Kimi-wa nani-o   naze katta-no
        you-top what-acc why bought Q
        'What did you buy why'

On the assumption that scrambling results in IP-adjunction, the S-structure seg-command relations are {naze < nani-o} in (46a) and {nani-o < naze} in (46b). Recall that in an adjoined structure like (43), y seg-commands z but z does not seg-command y.

In both (46a) and (46b) the chain of *naze* that links it to the +WH CP must be the primary one, for the usual ECP reason: so that antecedent government can hold in this chain. But in contrast to the English Superiority cases, (46a), where the wh-phrase of the primary chain *naze* commands the other wh-phrase, *nani-o* is ungrammatical, whereas (47b), with a wh-phrase (*nani-o*) that commands the wh-phrase in the primary chain, is well-formed. To extend his analysis to these cases, Watanabe makes the further assumption in (47):

(47) "*Condition on a Well-formed Wh-Phrase at LF*
     A pure wh-operator and the associate indeterminate phrase alone must form a category in order to function as a wh-phrase"
     (Watanabe 1991, 104).

Given (47), the LF CP-structure of (46a) must be as in (48), where *naze* adjoins to the empty operator lower than any other wh-element.

(48)

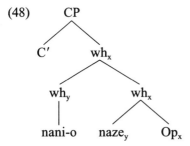

This representation violates (42): the IP-internal S-structure seg-command relation {naze < nani-o} has not been maintained. In (48) we have {nani-o < naze}.

Note that the crucial contrast between the English and the Japanese CP-structures is that the wh-phrase of the primary chain is in the head position of the spec-CP in English but adjoined to it in Japanese—the head of the spec position being occupied under Watanabe's analysis by the empty operator. Hence in the case of (46b) the IP-internal seg-command relation {nani-o < naze} is preserved at LF.

Again, there are certain problems with this analysis. First of all, the condition in (47) seems quite dubious. It results in a theory that requires the null spec-DP operator and its associate to form a constituent both at S-structure and at LF, but allows them to move separately. This seems to undesirably weaken the general correlation between movement/chain relations and constituenthood. Furthermore, (47) is necessary only to ensure within Watanabe's theory what seems to be simply an ECP effect, that in (48) *naze* adjoins first/lowest.

Let us then modify Watanabe's theory so that the necessity of adjoining *naze* first can be attributed to the ECP, while keeping the crucial English-Japanese difference that accounts for the different behavior of the two language types under Superiority: in English the first wh-phrase occupies the head position of spec-CP, while in Japanese the first wh-phrase is already adjoined to it. I have argued above against the hypothesis of empty spec-DP operator movement. Dispensing with this theory, we can still adopt Watanabe's assumption that an empty element fills the spec-(+WH)CP position in Japanese. Suppose that this element is inert with respect to determining an index for the ECP. We can take this state of affairs to force *naze* to adjoin in the lowest position to ensure that its index will percolate to spec-CP (so that spec-CP will provide the necessary antecedent for the adjunct trace).

Additional evidence for the claim that a category that is not in a movement/chain relation with an IP-internal position fills the spec-(+WH)CP position in Japanese is provided by Tonoiko (1991), although she in fact argues for Watanabe's null operator movement analysis. She takes the position that in embedded clauses the spec (+WH)CP position is filled by a nonempty operator, the element *ka*. This is a category that appears to function also as a coordinate conjunction, conjoining CPs in the case of *ka doo-ka*, she argues. She notes that in a yes-no question like (49) *ka* must be generated in CP since there is no argument to which it could be chain/movement related:

(49) Hare-te-i-mas-u   ka
      clear-TE-be-Pol-Prs KA
      'Is it clear/Has it cleared up'

(Tonoiko's evidence in support of Watanabe's overt spec-DP movement hypothesis involves distributional data like the contrast between (50a) and (50b):

(50) a. *Dare-ka/mo-ga-ka   ki-ta
        who-KA/MO-nom-KA come-Pst
     b. Dare/mo-ga ki-ta-ka
        'Did someone/everyone come'

(50a), with the phrase-final *ka* is ungrammatical, but (50b), with the clause-final *ka*, is fine. This would follow from the spec-DP (here *ka*) movement hypothesis which assumes that the movement is obligatory. But this is weak evidence, since we do not know a priori if the relation is of the movement/chain or of the construal (widely understood) type. Thus from the fact that in some language the structure corresponding to "the man Mary saw who" is ungrammatical, but "the man who Mary saw" is fine, no conclusion follows that the language must have overt Wh-movement. It could equally well have (empty) resumptive pronouns with a wh-phrase generated in situ in spec CP.)

The next problem with Watanabe's account of Superiority/Anti-superiority is that the relation-preservation condition (42) makes reference to more than one level of representation, that is, not only to LF but also to S-structure. No minimalist framework can assume such a principle. But it is easy to see that referring to S-structure is neither necessary nor sufficient for Watanabe's account to work. Crucially, he uses the distinction between IP-internal and CP-internal seg-command relations: IP-internal relations must be preserved CP-internally. Referring to levels of representations is not sufficient to make this distinction, since some wh-phrases can be in CP at S-structure. For example, in (44b) the relevant S-structure relation was between the trace of *what* and *who* rather than between *what* and *who* ("*?What did you persuade who to give t to Bill"). But once the necessary reference is made to the IP and the CP domain, referring to levels of representation becomes irrelevant, and thus the distinction can be made at LF.

The only remaining obstacle to adopting this modified version of Watanabe's analysis in the radical minimalist theory is his assumption that in-situ wh-phrases and associates raise to spec-CP at the level where relation preservation is checked. Eliminating this assumption is now trivial. Let us continue to suppose that empty scope markers are associated with in-situ wh-phrases. These scope markers are in spec-CP, and can occupy the same position the wh-phrases do in the LF representations of the standard Principles and Parameters theory. Thus the crucial difference between English and Japanese with respect to Superiority, that the lowest wh-phrase is adjoined to spec-CP only in the latter, can be equally well expressed in terms of empty scope markers associated with in-situ wh-phrases. The CP for (44b) will have the structure in (51), the CP of (46b) (52):

(51)

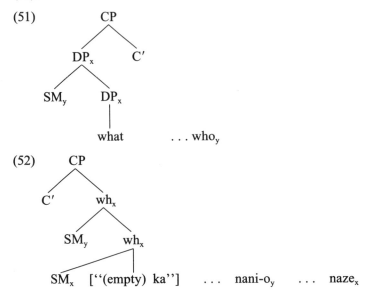

So if we require IP-internal seg-command relations to be preserved CP-internally and assume that the operator of the primary chain heads the DP in English but is adjoined to it in Japanese, we derive the same predictions as Watanabe, without the problems his theory encounters. This approach does not suffer from the problems of the spec-DP operator raising (multiple pied-piping mechanisms, ECP and Subjacency violations, necessity of condition (47)). It does not need to postulate multilevel conditions (like (42), which is incompatible with a minimalist approach). The LF raising of wh-associates/phrases, against which in a minimalist setting strong evidence exists from the binding theory, can also be dispensed with.

2.7 Conclusion

I have argued in this chapter, closely following Longobardi's (1991) treatment of negation in Italian, that all wh-chains are constrained by

Subjacency and that the secondary chains (of in-situ wh-phrases in English, for example) are parasitic on the primary chains that satisfy the Wh-Criterion requirement of the +WH C head. As in Longobardi's work, apparent lack of Subjacency effects were attributed (*a*) to the parasitic nature of the secondary chains and (*b*) to pied piping. The percolation possibilities of the [+wh] feature were parametrized; they were seen to be freer in Japanese and more restricted, though not nonexistent, in English and Italian. As expected within the radical minimalist theory, no distinction between S-structure and LF needed to be made with respect to the application of either Subjacency or pied piping.

I have also argued against Lasnik and Saito's (1992) claim that Subjacency must be a condition on rule application and against Fiengo et al.'s (1988) and Watanabe's (1991) solution to the LF Subjacency problem. Finally, I showed that the essential features of a version of Watanabe's account of Superiority are compatible with the LLF theory.

Chapter 3
Chains and D-Sets

3.1 Introduction

The central aim of this chapter is to provide an analysis of parasitic gap structures in terms of the Main Thematic Condition (MTC), repeated in (1), and to elaborate further on the notion of chain necessary for this account.

(1) *Main Thematic Condition*
    Only the root position(s) of a chain can be theta-related
    (i.e., assigning or receiving theta role).

Section 3.2 presents certain parasitic gap configurations that appear to be grammatical even though the primary gap c-commands the parasitic one. I introduce a version of E-Kiss's (1985) Case-matching requirement to account for the ungrammatical structures exhibiting this c-command configuration. In 3.3 I present and explain the adjunct argument asymmetry in these structures, originally noticed by Horvath (1992) in terms of the MTC. Section 3.4 discusses further the interaction of parasitic gap structures with principle C. Finally, in 3.5 I briefly consider chain composition and the possible existence of an empty operator associated with the parasitic gap.

As shown by Chomsky (1986a), the MTC is crucially involved in the explanation of Burzio's (1986) generalization. In the remainder of this introduction I shall briefly review the evidence for a UG that either includes the MTC or entails its effects in some other way by discussing the role the MTC plays in this explanation.

Let us start by considering examples (2a–c), which illustrate the case where a structure contains a chain with a non-root theta position; the chain in all three examples is (3). The root position of this chain is thematic in (2a) and (2b) and nonthematic in (2c):

(2) a. *John$_x$ hit t$_x$
   b. *John$_x$ considered t$_x$ to have met Mary
   c. *John$_x$ considered t$_x$ to seem that Mary left

(3) [John,t]

Example (3) is excluded by the MTC in (1): the position of *John*, a non-root position of the chain, is thematic. One might object that these examples are excluded also by Case-theoretical assumptions, namely the independently motivated principle in (4), or whatever (4) follows from.

(4) Only the head of an A-chain can be in a Case-position.

In the examples in (2), Case is assigned in both positions, resulting in a Case-conflict; (4) also correctly excludes chains where the unique Case-position is a non-head:

(5) a. *I tried John to hit t
   b. *I tried John to consider t to VP
   c. *I tried John to consider t to seem CP

In (5), as in (2), the relevant chain is (3). But here the head position of this chain is Caseless and only the non-head is in a Case position.

So one could apparently try to derive the effects of principle (1) from Case theory. The proponent of such an approach could point out that whenever a verb that has a complement assigns a theta role to its subject it generally assigns Case to its complement. The generalization is half of Burzio's (1986) principle, one statement of which is given in (6). (On the proviso that only structural Case is relevant, cf. Belletti 1988, Belletti and Rizzi 1988; Borer 1986; Lasnik 1992. For an explanation of the other conditional of Burzio's generalization, see Laka 1993.)

(6) A verb with a complement assigns a theta role to its subject iff it assigns (structural) Case to its complement.

The relevance of this part of Burzio's generalization is the following. Locality principles, presumably including the antecedent government requirement of the ECP, ensure that the two members of an A-chain link cannot be separated from each other by more than one head. In other words, if one member of this chain is in a complement position of a head H, then the next one must be in the subject position of H, as in (2a) and (5a). If the lower member is in a subject position, head-governed by a head H', then the next one must be in the subject position of H', as in

(2b,c) and (5b,c). Burzio's generalization ensures then that if a head assigns a theta role in its subject position to the higher member of a chain-link, this head will also assign Case to the lower member, which it necessarily governs, as either a complement or the governed subject of a complement. Thus if a chain including a given link [A,B] is excluded by (1) because A is a theta position, it will also be excluded by (4), since B will necessarily be a Case position.

Given Burzio's generalization, the effects of (1) will generally follow from the Case-theoretical principle in (4). However, as Chomsky's (1986a) discussion makes clear, an approach that derives (1) from the Case-theoretical principle in (4) is quite unlikely to be correct, because it must state Burzio's generalization independently in order to use it in the derivation of the effects of (1). But Burzio's generalization is a very unlikely candidate for a primitive of the theory. It refers to both Case and theta-theory at the same time and establishes a link that appears to be accidental and stipulative. As a postulate of the theory, it would be unique in its ability to relate these two subtheories, whose modular, encapsulated nature seems otherwise quite well established. Adopting Burzio's generalization as a primitive would therefore appear undesirable since it would weaken the claim of modularity of Case and theta theory. More generally this would weaken the predictive power of UG, since a theory that excludes such connections between modules is clearly more restrictive than one that does not.

This leads to the conclusion that rather than using Burzio's generalization in deriving (1), we should turn the argument around and, following Chomsky (1986a), attempt to explain the lexical regularity observed by Burzio in terms of the principle in (1). Let us consider, then, a verb V that violates Burzio's generalization: it assigns no Case to a category it governs—a complement of V or a subject of a complement of V that is governed by V—but assigns a theta role to its own subject. This would be a verb like *hit*, except that it assigns no Case to its object, as in (7a). Or equivalently, a verb like *appear* or a predicate like *was hit* but with a theta role assigned in subject position, as in (7b). In (7c) we have a verb like *believe* but one that assigns no Case to the embedded subject that it governs. Again, we could say equivalently that this is a verb like *seem*, except that it assigns a theta role to its subject, as in (7d):

(7) a. *John HIT t
    b. *John APPEARED t

   c. *John BELIEVED t to meet Mary
   d. *John SEEMS t to meet Mary

Such natural language predicates do not exist, as Burzio's generalization states.

Consider the position governed by these predicates: that of the object or the subject of the complement. This position is Caseless by hypothesis. Again we have an independently necessary Case-theoretical chain property that is relevant, namely (8):

(8) Only the non-head of an A-chain can be in a governed and Caseless position.

That is, heads of A-chains are either ungoverned (PRO) or in a Case-position (see, e.g., Chomsky 1986a; Brody 1985; Chomsky and Lasnik 1993 for discussion and different explanations). It follows that the position governed by H must be the lower member in some chain link [A,B]. Given the locality constraints alluded to above, the higher member, A, of this link can only be the subject of H. Thus in (7) the chain must be [John,t]. But A (*John*) is in a theta position by hypothesis again; hence the link is excluded by (1). In other words, verbs violating Burzio's generalization cannot exist, as a consequence of (1) (together with locality and Case-theory).

Recently Boskovic (1993) argued that the MTC does not hold in all cases. He claimed that in certain restructuring constructions, movement to theta position is possible.

(9) a. A Juan le quiere gustar Marta
     to Juan cl wants to like Marta
     'Juan wants to like Marta.'
  b. Ne vorrebbero   arrivare molti alla festa
     of them would want to arrive many to the party

Both of these examples appear to involve movement to the matrix subject position to which the verb assigns a theta role. The problematic nature of (9b) was originally noted in Burzio 1986. In both cases there are apparently dialects in which the equivalent of *want* behaves as a control verb: the thematic subject of *want* appears to be *Juan* in (9a) and *molti (ne)* in (9b). In (9a) the quirky Case on the subject suggests strongly that it is chain-related to the embedded clause where this Case could have been assigned—the matrix verb cannot assign dative. In (9b) *ne*-cliticization shows that a chain-relation exists between the matrix subject and the embedded ergative object; as Burzio showed, *ne*-cliticization is possible only from object position.

Boskovic accounts for the ungrammaticality of cases like (7a,b) by assuming that movement must always cross a maximal projection. Given the VP-internal subject hypothesis, movement to the thematic spec-VP position from the object position in this VP will then be impossible. As for (7c,d), he claims that these constitute cases of improper movement. Given some version of the requirement that clauses must have subjects (the EPP), movement from spec-VP must have proceeded through spec-IP before reaching the higher thematic spec-VP position. Given the EPP, it will then have to proceed further from matrix spec-VP to matrix spec-IP. Thus the movement in these cases will create nontheta-theta-nontheta chains, which are excluded on Boskovic's assumptions about improper movement.

Consider next the examples in (9), which are intended to demonstrate that movement to theta positions is in fact possible. Boskovic's assumption is that heads in restructuring constructions take VP complements; hence movement from the lower VP to the spec of the next involves a theta-theta chain, and thus no improper movement.

But it is quite dubious to attribute the MTC to a conspiracy of principles (cf. Brody 1987). Furthermore, recall from chapter 1 that the condition prohibiting movement to theta positions generalizes to prohibit lexical contextual requirements from holding in non-root positions of chains (the Generalized Projection Principle). Restrictions on improper movement are clearly too restricted in scope to predict this wider generalization. Assuming the existence of VP-complementation is also problematic in the minimalist setting (cf. Starke 1994). There are also more technical problems: under a binary-branching analysis of the VP, subject and object can be separated by a maximal (VP-)projection. This means that a subject-object chain, like the one in (7a), would not violate any principle that excludes chains that do not cross any maximal projections.

Rather than rejecting the MTC/GPP, we could assume that the chains in (9) involve no non-root non-theta positions at all. Suppose that the chain linking the matrix subject position and the embedded VP-internal position in the examples in (9) skips the matrix spec-VP and directly connects the lower spec-VP to the matrix spec-IP. In (9a) we have an overt chain whose members are the matrix spec-IP, the embedded spec-VP, and the embedded experiencer position where dative is assigned. In (9b) there is a covert expletive-associate chain, with the nonlexical expletive pro in the matrix spec-IP, a trace in the embedded spec-VP, and the associate in the embedded object position. The fact that these chains are related to the subject theta role of the matrix verb can be attributed to the presence of a PRO element in the spec of the matrix VP controlled by this chain. Other cases Boskovic discusses can be dealt with in a parallel fashion. I will thus continue to assume that the MTC/GPP is valid in its full generality.

3.2 Parasitic Gaps Licensed by Subjects

Structures in which the appearance of a gap in a Case-marked A-position is contingent on the presence of another one—that is, parasitic gap structures—have been discussed widely in the literature (e.g., Taraldsen 1981; Engdahl 1983; Chomsky 1982). Consider a canonical example of this configuration in (10a):

(10) a.   Which book did you criticize t without reading e
      b.   Which book did you criticize t without reading it
      c.   *Which book did you criticize it without reading e

As (10b) and (10c) show, there is an asymmetry between the status of the two gaps in this construction: the first but not the second can be present in (10) when the other is absent. (Examples where only the gap in the adjunct is present are possible in some rather marginal cases; see, for example, Cinque 1991. I shall ignore these here.) This asymmetry makes the standard usage of calling the first gap, *t*, in (10a) the "primary" gap and the second, *e*, the "parasitic" one quite natural.

A property of parasitic gap structures usually taken to be central and characteristic is (11):

(11) Neither the primary nor the parasitic gap c-commands the other gap.

Chomsky (1986b) contains an inconclusive discussion of whether (11) holds. His discussion centers around the question of whether a direct object primary gap should be taken to c-command a parasitic gap in an adjunct, as in (10a), and a clausal complement, as in (12):

(12) Which men did the police warn t that they were about to arrest e

I shall touch on these cases later. But I shall take up the anti-c-command condition with the examples where Chomsky's discussion leaves off. Consider (13), where the primary gap is in a subject position:

(13) a. Who did you believe [t to have visited Bill [before we talked to e]]
     b. Who did you believe [t visited Bill [before we talked to e]]

Examples like (13) have a marginal status, worse than standard parasitic gap configurations like (10a) but better than most parasitic gaps c-commanded by subject gaps. In fact, it is generally assumed that subject gaps do not license parasitic gaps (example (14)) except when the requirement in (11) is met, and neither of the gaps c-commands the other (example (15)).

(14) *Which books were unavailable before Mary read e

(15) Which books did John decide [before Mary read e] to tell his secretary t were unavailable

Notice that these examples all violate the requirement that the adjunct containing the parasitic gap be non-tensed, making them somewhat marginal. But examples like (13) seem at least marginally better than (14). Could it be that the acceptability of (13) is due to the option of interpreting the *before*-adjunct as part of the matrix clause? If the adjunct is not taken to be in the embedded clause, then of course the anti-c-command condition would not be violated. In (16) I control for this possibility: here the adjunct must be in the lower clause, as indicated by the interpretation.

(16) a. ?Who did Bill believe [t to have visited you [without you having invited e]]
     b. ?Who did Bill believe [t visited you [without you having invited e]]

Interestingly, (16) seems better than (13) in spite of the fact that the ambiguous attachment of the adjunct in (13) is resolved and the parasitic gap in the adjunct is clearly c-commanded by the embedded subject. This suggests that the main problem with (13) is not the violation of the anti-c-command condition but the tensed nature of the adjunct containing the parasitic gap. What goes on, then, in examples like (16); why are these better than (14) even though (14) and (16) appear equally to violate the anti-c-command condition (11)?

An observation of E-Kiss (1985) concerning Hungarian parasitic gap configurations points towards a solution. E-Kiss notes that there is a Case-matching requirement on parasitic gap configurations shown in Hungarian by minimal pairs like the following:

(17) a. *Kik   szeretnéd t ha t eljönnének anélkül   hogy
        Who(NOM) you'd-like if   came   without-it that
        meghivtál volna e
        you-had-invited
        'Who would you like if came without you having invited'
     b. Kiket   szeretnél t ha t eljönnének anélkül   hogy
        Who(ACC) you'd-like if   came   without-it that
        meghivtál volna e
        you-had-invited
        'Who would you like if came without you having invited'

In (17) we have a primary gap in the subject position of the embedded clause, and a parasitic gap in the adjunct. The primary gap is associated with a wh-phrase via an intermediate trace in the CP of the lower clause. Case assignment to this intermediate empty category by the matrix verb is possible in Hungarian. This is due to Case-assignment by the matrix verb to the spec-CP position of the wh-chain. Such Case assignment takes place in (17b), where the wh-phrase inherits the accusative assigned in the embedded CP by the matrix verb, which correspondingly shows indefinite object agreement, but not in (17a), where this Case assignment option is not taken. The important point to observe concerning (17) is that since (17a) and (17b) are a minimal pair differing only in Case properties, they demonstrate the existence of an additional constraint on parasitic gap formation.

E-Kiss argues that in parasitic gap configurations the Case of the A′-binder and that of the parasitic gap must match. Nakajima (1986, 1990) points out that this cannot hold in general, given the acceptability of parasitic gap structures of the following type:

(18) a man who whenever I meet e t looks old

In (18) the wh-phrase is associated with a primary gap in a nominative and a parasitic gap in an accusative Case position. The relevant difference between (18) and (17) appears to be precisely in the property we have been interested in throughout: c-command of the parasitic gap by the primary gap in (17) and lack of such c-command in (18). So it appears that E-Kiss's Case-matching requirement holds just where the parasitic gap is c-commanded by the primary gap. I shall assume that a Case-matching condition between the parasitic gap and the A′-antecedent of the primary gap is indeed necessary in such cases on the basis of the clear contrast in grammaticality between (17a) and (17b).

There are now two reasons for the ungrammaticality of (14): (11) and E-Kiss's Case-matching requirement. To allow (16) it is necessary to assume that accusative Case is assigned either to the primary gap or to some intermediate empty category connecting the primary gap to its antecedent. In the ECM construction (16a), Case is assigned to the primary gap; in (16b) this must have occured in spec-CP position. In both structures the Case is assigned by the matrix verb *believe*. Thus the Case-matching requirement is met in (16): the wh-phrase inherits accusative from a trace and this accusative matches the Case of the parasitic gap. There are then not one but two relevant differences between (14) and (15): (14) violates both (11) and E-Kiss's Case-matching condition but (15) violates neither.

Both (14) and (16) therefore violate the anti-c-command condition, but only (14) violates the Case-matching requirement. As we have just seen, in (16) the Case-matching condition is satisfied. But there is a distinction in acceptability between (14) and (16). This suggests that it is the Case-matching requirement that causes the strong ungrammaticality of (14), not the anti-c-command condition. In effect, the contrast between (14) and (16) might be on a par with the contrast between (17a) and (17b).

If the examples in (16) are worse than (15), then a violation of (11) by the adjunct-internal parasitic gap can be taken to cause only a mild degree of ungrammaticality. If they are on a par with (15), then (11) is simply irrelevant here altogether. Horvath (1992), who first presented Hungarian and English examples like (16) with the observation that in these the anti-c-command condition is violated, assumes that examples like (16) are as grammatical as standard parasitic gap structures. I shall tentatively make the same assumption.

3.3 Adjunct Versus Argument-Internal Parasitic Gaps

Horvath notes also that adjunct and argument-internal parasitic gaps behave differently with respect to the anti-c-command condition (11). While a violation of this condition by an adjunct internal parasitic gap results in relatively mild unacceptability, violation of (11) by an argument-internal gap is strongly ungrammatical:

(19) a. *Which girl did you expect t to meet everyone who liked e
　　 b. *Which girl did you expect t met everyone who liked e

The examples in (19a,b) can satisfy E-Kiss's Case-matching condition in the same way as the grammatical (16a,b): through ECM and Case-assignment in the spec of CP, respectively. Thus we have the following problem: if we appeal to (11) to explain the strong ungrammaticality of (19), why are the examples in (16) not just as fully ungrammatical? If, on the other hand, we take the violation of (11) to produce only mild or no ungrammaticality, then we have no condition to exclude (19).

A solution to this dilemma is provided by the MTC, given certain assumptions about the chain structure in parasitic gap structures. Suppose that chains do not have to partition the set of positions in the tree. In other words, assume that although all positions must belong to some chain and chains must be maximal, a given position may belong to more than one chain (cf. Chomsky 1986a for some discussion of this possibility). Under these hypotheses, the chain structure of a standard parasitic gap structure will be like (20) (ignoring intermediate traces):

(20) [Which book,   t]
     [Which book,   pg]

Both chains satisfy the MTC: no non-root position in either is thematic.

Consider in this light the problem of the contrasting behavior of adjunct-internal and argument-internal parasitic gaps, as in (16)—repeated here as (21)—and (19).

(21) a. ?Who did Bill believe [t to have visited you [without you having invited e]]

     b. ?Who did Bill believe [t visited you [without you having invited e]]

Assume that the thematic position of subjects is VP-internal (Kitagawa 1987; Koopman and Sportiche 1991; Manzini 1983, etc.), and that the sentential adjunct that contains the parasitic gap in (21) is either adjoined to the VP or to some higher head—in either case higher than the VP-internal trace of the primary gap. The object relative clause will of course be VP-internal. The structure of (21) and (19) will then be (22) and (23), respectively. Here t^1 is the trace in the non-thematic subject position and t^2 is the trace in the thematic position of the VP.

(22) wh-phrase$_x$ t^1_x $[_{VP}$ t^2_x]   [pg_x]

(23) wh-phrase$_x$ t^1_x $[_{VP}$ t^2_x [pg_x]]

Given the assumption that chains are maximal, the chain structure in (22) is (24) and that of (23) is (25):

(24) wh-phrase t^1 t^2

wh-phrase t^1 pg

(25) wh-phrase t^1 t^2 pg

Since t^2 in (22) does not c-command the parasitic gap, these two elements cannot be in the same chain. Since chains are maximal and their positions not necessarily disjoint, the chains of both of these categories will also contain t^1 and the wh-phrase. On the other hand, t^2 in (23) does c-command the parasitic gap; hence by the assumption of maximality they must be part of the same chain.

The MTC, then, predicts the difference between examples like (19) and (21). It excludes (strongly) complement-internal parasitic gaps when these are c-commanded by a subject primary gap, since the thematic position corresponding to the subject gap c-commands the parasitic gap and therefore must be part of the same chain. This results in a chain with a unique root, as in (25), but where a non-root position is thematic. Adjunct-internal parasitic gaps c-commanded by a subject primary gap, on the other hand, are not ruled out by the MTC: only the surface non-thematic position of the primary gap c-commands the parasitic gap, not the thematic position corresponding to the subject gap. Thus we have the chains in (24), both of which obey the MTC: only the two root positions are thematic.

Chomsky 1986b contains a related tentative proposal: that "subchains of a composed chain satisfying the c-command requirement for links" (Chomsky 1986b, 63–64) must obey (a version of) the MTC. The approach pursued here is essentially in the same spirit. But notice that Chomsky 1986b contains at least four related but distinct notions here: movement, chain, composed chain and c-command subchains of a composed chain. The present approach attempts to keep only two of these: chain (corresponding to Chomsky's notion of c-command subchains of composed chains) and composed chain. A further difference is that I take chain composition not to be a parasitic-gap-specific process (see section 3.5).

Recall the explanation of the MTC proposed in chapter 1. I argued there that this condition follows from the GPP: projectional features can only involve the root positions of chains, in other words, the D-set. This principle in turn was attributed to the assumption that projectional features express relations between chains and that therefore they have to identify all positions of the chain to which they are assigned in order to be saturated. This entailed the GPP, once projectional feature percolation was taken to apply only upwards in the structure. If a projectional feature is assigned to a non-root position then it cannot be saturated, since it cannot identify positions lower in the chain. The account carries over apparently without complications to the concept of chains just outlined.

Some further evidence for the notion of chains developed here is provided by E-Kiss's Case-matching condition. Recall the discussion of (18): the Case-matching condition cannot hold generally for all parasitic gaps. But we can now simply take the condition to apply chain-internally, the optimal situation.

3.4   Principle C and the MTC Analysis of Parasitic Gaps

As discussed in section 3.2, a principle-C account of the anti-c-command condition on parasitic gap structures cannot distinguish the strongly ungrammatical subject-licensed parasitic gap structure (14), where E-Kiss's Case-matching requirement is violated, from the comparatively less unacceptable and perhaps grammatical (16), which involves no Case requirement violation. If principle C is taken to be violated in (14), repeated as (26), then it is violated also in (16), reproduced as (27):

(26)   *Which books t were unavailable before Mary read e

(27)   a.   Who did Bill believe [t to have visited you [without you having
             invited e]]

        b.   Who did Bill believe [t visited you [without you having invited
             e]]

Furthermore, as the previous section showed, an anti-c-command condition enforced by principle C could not predict Horvath's generalization. Such an approach cannot differentiate cases like (27), where the parasitic gap is inside an adjunct, from structures like (19), repeated as (28), where it is inside an argument.

(28)   a.   *Which girl did you expect t to meet everyone who liked e

        b.   *Which girl did you expect t met everyone who liked e

If principle C is taken to exclude (26) it will then exclude (26), (27), and (28) in a uniform fashion. The present account, in terms of two different but independently motivated principles, makes what appear to be the right distinctions: E-Kiss's Case-matching requirement excludes (26) and the MTC rules out (28), but neither of these conditions is violated by (27).

Further evidence for the MTC analysis of parasitic gaps is provided by Contreras's (1984) and Hudson's (1984) observations. Contreras argues that in examples like (29) the parasitic gap in the adjunct is c-commanded by the primary gap in object position.

(29) Which book did you criticize t before reading e

(30) a. We never saw him before we examined John Smith
        b. We never saw his parents before we examined John Smith

His argument is that the impossibility of coreference in (30a) between the name in the adjunct and the pronoun in the direct object position cannot be attributed simply to the fact that the example shows backwards pronominalization. This is because (30b) is much better than (30a) in spite of the fact that this sentence also involves backwards pronominalization. There appears to be only one relevant difference between (30b) and (30a): in (30b) the pronoun is more deeply embedded. This suggests quite strongly that principle C is responsible for the ungrammaticality of the coreferential reading of (30a).

The conclusion creates a contradiction in any system that uses principle C to account for the anti-c-command effects in parasitic gap configurations, but is of course unproblematic for the theory defended here. Principle C might involve some weaker notion of c-command, m-command presumably; the definition of chain-roots that the MTC refers to can still be phrased in terms of the stricter notion of c-command. Thus the MTC is observed by (29) but principle C is violated by (30a).

Similar comments apply to the type of example in (31), noted by Engdahl (1984) and Hudson (1984):

(31) Which men did the police warn t that they were about to arrest e

Suppose that the clausal complement in this type of example is taken to be extraposed into a VP-adjoined position (Chomsky 1986b; Browning 1987). The matrix object will then weakly but not strongly c-command all positions inside the embedded sentence, allowing the parasitic gap structure but predicting also the contrast in (32) if principle C uses the weaker notion of c-command.

(32) a. *The police warned them$_x$ that they were about to arrest those men$_x$
        b. The police warned their$_x$ parents that they were about to arrest those men$_x$

Lasnik and Stowell (1991) attribute the contrast between the grammaticality of the parasitic gap structure in (29) and the case of object-bound

R-expression (30a) to the assumption that the parasitic gap has the status of an epithet, a definite description that functions like a pronoun. They note that epithets like *the bastard* in (33) generally observe principle C, as exemplified in (33a) and (33b), but claim that an object-bound epithet, as in (33c), is more acceptable than an object-bound R-expression (33d):

(33) a. *John$_x$ was told that the bastard$_x$ was unwelcome
      b. *John$_x$ kicked Mary before the bastard$_x$ grabbed her
      c. Mary kicked John$_x$ before the bastard$_x$ had a chance to grab her
      d. ??Mary discovered them$_x$ before John had read the papers$_x$

Lasnik and Stowell's examples are not ideal for testing this claim. In (33d) the name is bound by a pronoun, whereas in (33c) the epithet is bound by a name. But once we control for this difference it is not clear that a contrast remains:

(34) a. Mary kicked John$_x$ before the bastard$_x$ had a chance to grab her
      b. Mary kicked John$_x$ before John$_x$ had a chance to grab her
      c. Mary kicked him$_x$ before the bastard$_x$ had a chance to grab her
      d. Mary kicked him$_x$ before John$_x$ had a chance to grab her

In (34a,b) a proper name is the antecedent of both the epithet and the proper name; in (34c,d), a pronoun. There is a minor difference in acceptability between (34a) and (34b), but this can be attributed to the weak pragmatic prohibition against the repetition of the proper name. In both (34c) and (34d) the coreferential reading seems fairly accessible; apparently the effect of principle C in the case of object-bound elements can be overridden, presumably by pragmatic considerations. But there appears to be little contrast between (34c) and (34d). The examples thus do not appear to provide evidence for the claim that principle C should ignore object positions just in the case of epithets.

3.5 Chain Composition, Empty Operators

Given the close parallels between absorbed multiple wh- and parasitic-gap constructions, we would expect the parasitic gap to be a contentive element parallel to the wh-in-situ. Further, we expect it to be associated with a scope marker parallel to the scope marker of the wh-in-situ in multiple wh-constructions. The scope marker should be in the spec of the same head where the wh operator of the primary gap is, adjacent to the operator of the primary chain, as in (35).

(35) SM Who did Bill believe [t to have visited you [without you having invited e]]

We can assume that essentially the same chain composition/absorption process applies both in absorbed multiple-wh-type structures and in parasitic-gap constructions. (Absorption is necessary to account for the interpretation, while chain composition appears to be necessary to account for the locality properties of these constructions; cf. Kayne 1983; Chomsky 1986b; Frampton 1990; Manzini 1993, among others.) When applying in the parasitic-gap construction, absorption will presumably create a quantifier composed of the scope marker and the wh-operator, the element that will then be the head of both the parasitic and the primary chains. In this way the dedicated parasitic-gap-specific chain-composition process is avoided.

Further suggestive evidence for the parallelism between multiple-wh-structures and parasitic-gap constructions is provided by those dialects where certain multiple-gap structures are ambiguous between a multiple question and a standard parasitic gap interpretation. In such as dialect (36a,b) can also be understood as anticipating answers like (37a,b) respectively. (Cf. Clark 1983; Lasnik and Stowell 1991.)

(36) a. (SM)Who did your stories about e upset t
     b. (SM)Who did you give your pictures of e to t

(37) a. My stories about Bob upset Bill
     b. I gave my pictures of Bob to Bill

The difference between the two interpretations of (36) can be attributed to the index of the empty scope marker: coindexed with the overt wh-phrase under the standard interpretation, and in certain configurations optionally bearing a different index in the more permissive dialect.

There is some evidence for the claim that contrary to the proposed analysis, parasitic gaps are associated with an empty operator that intervenes between the parasitic gap and the primary chain. A well-known asymmetry in the behavior of the primary and the parasitic gap, noted by Kearney (1983), seems difficult to handle in a theory in which both gaps are bound by the same operator. Anaphor reconstruction is possible only into the primary gap position:

(38) a. Which books about himself did John file t before Mary read e

    b. *Which books about herself did John file t before Mary read e

Given a parasitic-gap-associated empty operator intervening between the parasitic gap and the primary chain, the distinction between (38a) and (38b) can be made as in Chomsky 1986b: reconstruction is not permitted to apply across this element.

Browning (1987) raises a problem for this account, that reconstruction across an operator is possible in the adjectival complement construction:

(39) This picture of himself is easy [Op [to make John to buy e]]

In (39) *John* is a legitimate antecedent of the anaphor, showing reconstruction of the matrix subject into the position of the empty category. Browning notes also that such reconstruction is not always possible:

(40) a. *Mary expected those pictures of himself to be easy [Op [to make John to buy e]]

    b. Mary said that those pictures of himself are easy [Op [to make John to buy e]]

The generalization appears to be that reconstruction across an operator is possible only if no "closer" obligatory antecedent is available for the anaphor, as is the case in (39) and (40b) but not in (40a) or (38b). Thus, although these examples raise some doubts about the relevance of the empty operator, this element still appears to play a role.

It is not clear, however, if the generalization should also cover parasitic gap structures in addition to adjectival complements like (39) and (40) and other similar constructions. Given the approach adopted here, where the parasitic gap is a contentive element we expect reconstruction into it to be impossible in any case.

Another asymmetry was pointed out by Lasnik and Stowell (1991): parasitic gaps do not trigger weak crossover (WCO) violations:

(41) Who$_x$ did you gossip about t$_x$ [[despite his$_x$ teacher's having vouched for e$_x$]]

(42) Which man$_x$ is [[everyone who asks his$_x$ wife about e$_x$]] usually interested in t$_x$

Under Lasnik and Stowell's analysis, parasitic gaps are bound by a null operator that is not a "true quantifier," that is, one that does not range over any nonsingleton set, and which furthermore does not bind the primary gap. Following the approach of Sportiche (1983) they then assume that a locally A'-bound empty category triggers WCO effects only if it is bound by a true quantifier. They take an empty category to be an epithet if it is locally A'-bound by an operator that is not a true quantifier. But again we could assume that the contentive parasitic gap is an epithet without postulating a distinct null operator for it. (See Postal 1993 for data that raises problems for the standard analyses of WCO and for Lasnik and Stowell's account of the disappearance of WCO effects in the constructions they discuss.)

There is some apparent evidence also from principle C for an intervening empty operator. On the assumption that examples like (16)/(27) are grammatical (or if they are not, then this is not due to principle C), principle C plays no role in determining the patterning of parasitic-gap configurations. The question is then how to ensure that principle C does not exclude the configuration where a primary gap c-commands the parasitic one. If an operator were present in these structures in a position where it c-commanded the parasitic but not the primary gap, then the structure of (27a) would be like (43):

(43) Who did Bill believe [t to have visited you [Op [without you having invited e]]]

Principle C would not exclude this configuration, even though a c-command relationship holds between the primary and the parasitic gap, given its standard proviso: principle C restricts elements only in the domain of their associated operator.

I shall assume instead that principle C refers to chains, not categories. Thus it regulates only the relations between chains, it does not operate chain internally (see also Barrs 1986 for a similar assumption within a different approach). This makes an intervening empty operator in parasitic gap structures unnecessary. Note that improper movement constructions cannot then be excluded as in May 1979 by principle C (cf. Brody 1993 for a Case-theoretical account). (Note also that the restriction of principle C to the domain of the associated operator—or some alternative like the one in terms of predication in Lasnik and Stowell 1991—is not made redundant by this interpretation of the condition; it is still necessary to avoid excluding structures like the purposive "John bought a dog [Op [PRO to play with t].")

In sum, the evidence for the existence of a parasitic-gap-associated intervening operator can be accounted for in other ways. (The assumption that this element appears at an intervening position, at the island boundary containing the parasitic gap (Chomsky 1986b), is problematic in any case, since there appears to be no appropriate landing site for it there. See, e.g., Hoekstra 1988. More recent theories that address the locality problems of the construction therefore tend to dispense with such an operator; cf. Frampton 1990; Manzini 1993.)

3.6 Conclusion

In this chapter I have discussed the adjunct-argument asymmetry in those parasitic-gap structures where a primary subject gap c-commands the parasitic one. In such structures, parasitic gaps inside adjuncts are grammatical, whereas those inside arguments are ill-formed. I assumed that arguments of the verb, but not adjuncts, are c-commanded by the VP-internal thematic subject position. The MTC then predicted the asymmetry once the concept of chain was characterized in the appropriate fashion. In the ill-formed configuration a non-root chain position is thematic, violating the MTC. Additional evidence for the analysis was provided by its resolution of certain problems associated with the principle-C-based explanation of the anti-c-command condition. Finally, the parallel treatment of parasitic-gap structures and multiple-wh constructions made it possible to eliminate the parasitic-gap-specific chain-composition process and the problematic intervening empty operator associated with the parasitic gap.

Chapter 4

Positional Principles

4.1 Introduction

The concept of chains is different from that of Move α. A chain simply expresses a relationship, between a set of positions or categories. The rule of Move α, besides expressing the same relation, embodies the claim that a category can occur in different positions during the derivation. These positions may be at different levels of representation in the structural description of a sentence, as in the standard Principles and Parameters theory analysis, or they may be part of the derivation of the sole syntactic level of representation, as in the derivational minimalist framework.

In theories that assume Move α, this rule and constraints on its application are instrumental in ensuring that categories are in the appropriate position in structural descriptions. The radical minimalist theory that rejects Move α will have to be different in two respects. First, a category cannot change its position either at different levels of representation or during the derivation of *the* syntactic level. Second, chain-theoretical principles will have to replace those conditions on the application of Move α that constrain the distribution of traces and their antecedents.

These principles fall into two subclasses. In the first class are those restrictions that constrain the establishment of relationships of the type expressed by chains and Move α, like Subjacency, ECP, and the shortest move principle. In the other class we have constraints that in the standard framework (including here the standard minimalist theory) have to do with the point of application of Move α, forcing the movement to be overt or to take place only in the post S-structure LF component. Principles like Chomsky's (1993) "Procrastinate" or Pesetsky's (1989) "Earliness" belong to this class.

In this chapter I look at the distribution of the lexical elements in various types of chains. Recall that in the radically minimalist framework the difference between LF and overt movement translates into the question of the position of the contentive (nonexpletive) category. "Overt movement" from position P/2 to position P/1 corresponds in this theory to a chain where the contentive element is in P/1, and "LF movement" to a chain where it is in P/2.

In section 4.2 I discuss the minimalist assumption that overt movement is triggered by "strong" features at PF. I argue that these features in fact should have effect at (L)LF—a conclusion that is incompatible with derivational frameworks but that makes sense in the radically minimalist theory put forward here. In 4.3 I discuss the "timing principles" on derivations. One of these is Procrastinate, the other a version of Earliness. Simplifying somewhat, Procrastinate prevents overt movement unless triggered at PF; Earliness forces overt movement unless prevented by lack of S-structure licensing of some position involved. I argue that there are various reasons to prefer an approach in terms of Earliness to one invoking Procrastinate. But Earliness seems difficult to reconcile with economy principles and is conceptually problematic for that reason. I show that this problem can also be resolved in the radical minimalist framework by substituting a principle of (L)LF-PF Transparency, the representational equivalent of Earliness.

In section 4.4 I look at "LF movement" from A'-positions and offer an analysis in terms of the Transparency condition. I argue that certain aspects of the analysis cannot be restated in terms of the standard derivational theory. Finally, in 4.5 I discuss the status of the rule of Quantifier raising and the problem of antecedent-contained ellipsis.

4.2   PF-Triggering versus LLF-Triggering

Let us assume, following the Emonds-Pollock type analysis, that in tensed clauses French main verbs are in the Infl position, while the English Infl category is under V. (Since the split-inflection hypothesis is generally irrelevant to my concerns here, for simplicity of presentation I shall often refer to Infl where it might be more precise to talk about some constituent of Infl, like Agr or Tns.) As exemplified in (1) this accounts for, among other things, the different relative position of the adverb and the verb in French and English on the hypothesis that the (relevant type of) adverb is invariably placed between Infl and the VP nodes:

(1) a. John Infl   often   eat + s spaghetti
    b. Jean embrass + e souvent V   Marie

(2) a. *John eat + s often   V   spaghetti
    b. *Jean Infl   souvent embrass + e Marie

It remains to account for the impossibility of (2a) and (2b): V under Infl in English and Infl under V in French. Consider Chomsky's (1993) checking-theory solution. Instead of assuming a process of Infl-lowering in English, he adopts a checking theory of inflection. Thus the verb is taken to insert from the lexicon together with its inflectional features, and these features will have to match the features generated under the Infl node. Checking of the verbal inflectional features by Infl can take place only when the verb together with its inflectional features has raised to Infl, overtly in French, in the LF component in English. Infl lowering is now unnecessary.

To account for the obligatoriness of verb raising in the French case, Chomsky adopts Pollock's (1989) distinction between "weak" and "strong" Infl nodes and suggests that in French the verb has to raise overtly because the strong Inflection of French has to check the inflectional features of the verb at PF. The mechanism and rationale is that those features of Infl that have successfully participated in checking delete. Strong but not weak features are visible (or, alternatively, only weak features are freely deletable) at PF. Full Interpretation (FI) is then violated if any (visible) features of Infl are present at PF. Strong features are thus forced to check and delete in the overt syntax. In this way the ungrammaticality of (2b) is accounted for: since overt movement of the verb + inflection complex has not taken place, the strong Infl could not check the inflectional features by PF and thus is still present at this level, where it violates FI.

To account for the impossibility of (2a), Chomsky invokes the principle of "Procrastinate"—"a natural economy condition: LF-movement is 'cheaper' than overt movement." "The system tries to reach PF 'as fast as possible,' minimizing overt syntax" (Chomsky 1993, 30–31). Thus in the English case overt raising is not forced by FI; by Procrastinate it is therefore not possible. The account is generalized to A- and A'-movement. These take place overtly when triggered by a "strong" feature (like the Q-features of C or the N-features of Infl) that needs to check and delete by PF. When not so triggered, the movement can take place only in the LF component by Procrastinate.

The innovations of the checking theory of inflection thus include crucially the PF triggering of overt movement and the Procrastinate principle. There are some reasons to question both of these. Postponing discussion of Procrastinate until the next section, consider first the assumption of PF triggering of overt movement. Since PF and LF are independent levels, it is a surprising accident that for those morphemes whose features have to be checked at PF (i.e., have strong features) an exactly identical requirement holds at both LF and PF. Optimally this identity relation should be captured, but even minimally, the theory should be constructed in a way that does not make this relation necessarily a curious accident. Thus the fact that strong features have identical effects at both LF and PF clearly suggests that these requirements hold at the same level of representation.

This problem is highlighted by the case of multiple overt Wh-movement constructions, exemplified by the Hungarian structure in (3):

(3) Ki   kit   t   szeret t
    who-nom who-acc likes
    'Who likes who'

Movement of the first wh-phrase in (3) can be attributed to a requirement of the +WH X^0 node, readily formulable in terms of the PF-triggering theory. However, obligatory overt movement of the other wh-phrases is then unexpected, indeed prohibited under Procrastinate, contrary to fact. (See Pesetsky 1989 and Epstein 1991 for discussions of this type of construction in the context of Chomsky's earlier (1991) theory.)

Cheng (1991) provides a solution that makes such data compatible with Procrastinate. She argues that here an independent requirement is at work. Procrastinate does not prevent multiple Wh-movement because this is due to a requirement on the wh-phrases: their wh feature needs to be licensed by a +WH C node. She assumes that these wh-phrases contain a pro element that needs to be identified in Chomsky's (1982) and Rizzi's (1986b) sense by a +WH C node. Identification is local, forcing all wh-phrases to move. Multiple Wh-movement then appears not to be a problem for Procrastinate: all wh-phrases are forced to move.

Within Cheng's theory this licencing mechanism in effect appears to lead to circularity. She assumes also that in a language containing no question particle the +WH C must be licensed/typed as +WH by a moved wh-phrase (see below). If the wh-phrases (containing pro) can be licensed/identified as wh by the +WH C, then in a multiple Wh-movement language that contains no question particle the source of the +WH/ wh feature is unclear. The circularity is created by the fact that Cheng appears to take both licencing mechanisms here to involve some kind of content-identification (as +WH/wh). To avoid this, let us transplant Cheng's analysis of multiple Wh-movement into the minimalist framework. Suppose that the wh feature of wh-phrases in multiple Wh-movement languages is strong and needs to be licensed/checked in a spec-head configuration by a +WH C node, forcing overt movement. The circularity is now avoided, a strong +WH C and a strong wh-phrase can mutually license/check each other.

Cheng's analysis, whether in its original or in its modified form, brings into focus the dubious aspect of the PF-triggering theory of overt movement just noted. PF triggering by strong features duplicates a subset of LF triggering configurations, raising doubts about the assumption that strong features need to be satisfied at the phonological level. Cheng's account of multiple Wh-movement rescues Procrastinate at the price of having to claim that in multiple Wh-movement languages the strong feature of wh-phrases forces all of them to be in a spec-head configuration with a +WH C at S-structure (so that the feature is checked by PF). At the same time, the strong +WH feature of C forces such a head to be in a spec-head configuration with a wh-phrase. Thus these strong features at PF enforce one or the other clause of the LF Wh-Criterion by S-structure. But the Wh-Criterion has nothing to do with phonology. So the fact that triggering by strong features needs to fully duplicate the Wh-Criterion suggests strongly that such triggering in fact takes place at (L)LF, the natural location for this principle.

Within the derivational minimalist theory, the assumption that a strong feature triggers movement at LF only would of course fail to ensure that such movement takes place overtly, feeding PF. Within the present theory, however, this assumption creates no problems—indeed, this is exactly what is expected. Since in this theory a category is in a position at LLF that corresponds to its PF position if strong features force an element to be in position P at LF, it will be in the position that corresponds to P also at PF. The radically minimalist theory has to answer the converse question, though: why do weak features not force "overt movement"? If weak features also must be satisfied at LF, then what is the difference between these and strong features? But within the proposed framework there is a straightforward answer: weak features can be satisfied by chains, whereas strong features can only be satisfied by categories.

For a concrete example, consider the English multiple wh-construction in (4) (recall that SM is the expletive empty category interpreted in wh-constructions as a scope marker):

(4) $[_{CP}$ SM$_x$ who$_y$ C $[_{IP}$ t$_y$ saw what$_x$ $]]$

There is no level in the radical minimalist theory where a wh-in-situ is in spec-CP position, thus no level where the requirement that all wh-phrases must be in the spec of a +WH CP holds. The constraint remains valid, however, when restated in terms of chains. Thus it still is the case that all wh-phrases must be in some chain whose head is in a spec position of a +WH C. Let us reformulate the wh-criterion (May 1985, Rizzi 1991) accordingly:

(5) *The Wh-Criterion*
   a. A +WH C must have the head of a chain that contains a
      wh-phrase in its spec position.
   b. A wh-phrase must be in a chain whose head is in the spec of a
      +WH C.

Thus (5) is a universal requirement at LF. Note that condition (5a) does not require the wh-phrase to be in the head position of its chain in a direct spec-head relation with the +WH C. A structure like (6a), where the wh-phrase remains in situ but forms a chain with an empty operator in spec-CP, satisfies the requirements in (5):

(6) a. *I wonder SM$_x$ C Mary saw who$_x$
    b. I wonder who$_x$ C Mary saw t$_x$

If English +WH C is strong, however, this will force the LLF structure in (6b) on the assumption that strong features can only be checked by the appropriate categories themselves. Similarly, the Hungarian multiple-wh structure in (7) satisfies the wh-criterion. But if the wh-phrases have a strong feature (as in Cheng's theory) that needs to be checked by LLF, then both wh-phrases will have to be in the head position of their respective chains at this level and therefore also at PF, as in (7b). (But cf. section 4.3 for a different account. Also, (7a) may be acceptable when the wh-in-situ is taken with a specific interpretation—perhaps D-linked in the sense of Pesetsky (1987). I ignore problems connected with D-linking here.)

(7) a. *SM$_x$ Ki$_y$ t$_y$ hozott   mit$_x$
            who-nom brought what-acc
         'Who brought what'

b. Ki$_y$ mit$_x$ t$_y$ hozott t$_x$
   who-nom what-acc brought
   'Who brought what'

To sum up: in the standard minimalist theory, morphemes with strong features have identical requirements at LF and PF levels—a surprising accident. The fact that these requirements correlate, unexpected if they hold at different interface levels, points toward a theory, like the one put forward here, where both weak and strong features take effect at the same level of representation. Such a theory can explain why PF and LF requirements appear to correlate in the standard minimalist theory. Since the two requirements hold at the same level, the assumption that they are essentially identical creates no problems of principle. Weak and strong features will of course continue to differ in that the former can be satisfied by chains, the latter only by categories.

4.3   Earliness and LF-Triggering

Consider next Procrastinate. One problem with this principle is that it seems to be incompatible with Greed, the condition that elements move only in order to satisfy their own requirements (Chomsky 1993). According to Greed, movement of a category never takes place solely in order to satisfy a requirement of some other element in the structure. Greed is a natural and desirable restriction, and therefore the data that shows it to be incompatible with Procrastinate provides some evidence against the latter condition.

This incompatibility is not difficult to demonstrate. Take the assumption that overt Wh-movement is triggered by a strong feature that needs to be checked. This feature may in principle be either a feature of the wh-phrase or a feature of the +WH head into whose spec the wh-phrase moves. Multiple wh-constructions show that the strong feature cannot be that of the wh-phrase in English—if it were, then all wh-phrases would have to raise overtly. Thus, in the framework where the default is covert movement, or Procrastinate, and overt movement is triggered only by strong features, we must apparently conclude that Greed is violated. The wh-phrase raises in order to satisfy the requirement of another element, the +WH head. As Wilder and Cavar (1993) point out, this situation arises in general when an element must move in certain configurations but not in others. Another example that they provide is the case of V-movement in German V/2 configurations:

(8) a. Hans küßt Maria
        'Hans kisses Maria'
    b. *Hans Maria küßt

(9) a. ... daß Hans Maria küßt
        'that Hans kisses Maria'
    b. *... daß Hans küßt Maria

Again V-raising cannot occur because some feature of the verb is strong, since the verb would then have to raise in both matrix and embedded clauses. Hence if a strong feature triggers movement it must be a feature of the matrix C. But then V-raising violates Greed, since the verb raises to satisfy the requirements of a different element, namely the matrix C. Wilder and Cavar develop an account in terms of "early altruism," a notion that allows violations of Greed under certain circumstances. (See also Lasnik 1993 for the essentially identical concept of "enlightened altruism.")

But it is necessary to weaken Greed only if Procrastinate is taken to be part of the grammar. Suppose that we proceed instead in the spirit of Pesetsky's (1989) "Earliness" principle. Let us assume that movement must take place as early in the derivation as possible. This condition is opposite in spirit to Procrastinate. If movement must take place at some stage, and it can take place overtly, it will have to do so. Instead of assuming that overt movement is triggered (only) by strong features, let us assume that (only) strong features license overt movement. Such an approach immediately accounts for the overtness of a single wh-movement per +WH C in English if this head licenses a single wh-phrase in its spec position. Similarly, Earliness together with the assumption that in German only the matrix C licenses overt V-raising ensures that in this language the matrix verb and only the matrix verb raises to C overtly.

Given Earliness the problems with Greed disappear: no category needs to have moved in order to satisfy the requirements of some other element. There are other advantages. First, the approach to overt movement in terms of morphological triggering apparently cannot restrict triggers to those heads into whose projections movement takes place. Thus, as we have just seen in the case of multiple overt Wh-movement in Hungarian, it apppears necessary to assume that the strong feature in such constructions belongs to the moved element and not to the element moved to, as in the more standard cases. Under the Earliness approach, on the other hand, licensing can be uniformly a property of the heads moved to. The difference between English and Hungarian can reduce to the fact that in English the +WH head licenses only one wh-phrase, whereas in Hungarian it licenses more than one such category.

Another major problem with Procrastinate that Earliness will resolve is that the approach in terms of Procrastinate claims that in the default case LF will be maximally different from PF. According to Procrastinate, movement must take place covertly when overt movement is not triggered by the morphology. The prediction is then that grammars in which LF and PF are not made similar by morphological accidents are more highly valued. This is a strange consequence, which seems to contradict the spirit of the economy approach. Based on general considerations of economy we would expect exactly the opposite: that in the default case LF is maximally similar to PF, so that it can be recovered with the minimum of effort. And this is exactly what follows from the Earliness view of overt movement. (See Pollock 1993 for additional arguments for an Earliness-based approach.)

The principle of Last Resort, which requires that movement take place only when necessary, appears to contradict Earliness, which requires movement to take place as soon as possible. In fact, the contradiction is only apparent. Last Resort is not a timing principle; it contributes to determining whether movement, overt or covert, can take place at all. Earliness will only refer to cases of movement that are compatible with Last Resort, requiring them to be overt in the default case.

While no problems arise from the interaction of Earliness with the Last Resort principle, a serious problem still remains. Although in a different way than Procrastinate, Earliness also seems incompatible with the general economy maxim of achieving a given result with the minimum effort. As we have seen, Procrastinate has the dubious consequence that LF and PF are maximally different in the default case. If it did not have this consequence, Procrastinate would be a plausible economy principle: delaying some action as long as possible may result in not having to carry it out at all, since the requirement to act may cease to exist. But Earliness has exactly the opposite, unwanted, effect: Earliness will force an operation to take place that could become unnecessary at some later stage (Brody 1991b). Thus we have something approaching an internal contradiction in the derivational framework: neither Earliness nor Procrastinate can be straightforwardly reconciled with considerations of economy.

The problem does not arise within the radical minimalist theory. Recall that in this framework chains at the sole syntactic level of LLF express the type of relations captured in the standard theories primarily by Move α (and only derivatively by chains). Overt movement from position P/2 to P/1 corresponds to a contentive category in P/1, LF movement to one in P/2. We continue to assume the hypothesis that the position of the lexical category in its chain is a matter of morphology. Procrastinate corresponds to the assumption that the default position of the contentive is the root of its chain, P/2, while the Earliness view can be captured by taking the head position P/1 as the default position. Since no movement operation is involved, the only economy consideration is the one that disfavors a Procrastinate-type account, which claims that LF and PF tend to maximally differ. The problem with Earliness disappears, once no movement is taken to be involved: the question of avoiding an operation does not arise. This leads to the conclusion that we should take the default position of the contentive to be the head position of its chain. Let us call this assumption the principle of Transparency (cf. Lightfoot 1979 for an earlier proposal in the same spirit but in a different context):

(10) *Transparency*
      The contentive category in the chain must be in the highest position licensed by morphology.

Transparency is natural; the basic idea is to some extent shared by all relevant theories. The assumption that at (L)LF all contentives are in a high enough position to be in a local configuration (directly or through a trace) with the heads that have the relevant checking features (whether these features are strong or weak) is made also in the standard minimalist framework. The principle in (10) adds the proviso that the appearance of a contentive in a position other than the root of its chain must be morphologically licensed. (Recall from chapters 1 and 3 that for categories other than adjuncts the chain-root is the position involved in projection.) In the radically minimalist theory, where there is a common interpretive and lexical interface, the locus of this morphological licensing can only be this level: LLF.

Transparency can be taken to express the hypothesis that UG is built to maximize the recoverability of LLF from PF. The contentive must be as high as possible in the chain in order to make explicit the LLF chain relations at PF. The expressive power of the morphology of a particular language, however, may limit the ability of contentives to carry this information explicitly to the PF level. We can reasonably consider the principle of shortest distance to derive also from such Transparency considerations that require maximal recoverability of LLF chain relations from PF. Last Resort can also be reconstructed as a Transparency principle. Given a category in a position where it checks some feature F, by Last Resort its trace is restricted to positions where it cannot check F. Transparency principles will thus facilitate the construction of LLF from PF. Contentives tend to be in the head of their chain (by (10)), traces are local to their antecedent (by the shortest distance principle), and the position of the trace is further restricted: there must be some feature (of the contentive, by Greed) that cannot be checked here but is checked in the position of the antecedent (by Last Resort).

Given the motivation of the Transparency principle in (10) to maximize the recoverability of LLF chain structure from PF, it might appear unexpected that heads of chains are not necessarily lexically realized. Contentives can also be pronominal empty categories, PRO or *pro* in the case of XP chains. Since *pro* must be Case-marked (Rizzi 1986b, Chomsky 1993), it will carry a phonologically relevant feature that indicates its presence at PF. As for PRO, it is also sometimes taken to have a special "null" Case (cf. Chomsky and Lasnik 1993). If this approach is correct then the motivation given for (10) can generalize also to this element.

Let us again take wh-chains to exemplify the operation of the Transparency principle in (10). English and Japanese differ in that a +WH C in the former but not in the latter licenses a contentive wh-phrase in its spec position. In Japanese-type languages the +WH C licenses only an expletive element, a "pure" wh-operator, in the sense of Watanabe (1991) and Chomsky (1993). This may be an empty operator, as Watanabe proposes or a lexical element, as Tonoiko (1992) suggests. (Cf. the discussion above in chapter 2). The English +WH C can license only one wh-phrase, whereas in a multiple Wh-movement language like Hungarian it has the ability to license more than one. Notice that the relevant chain structure is universal: all wh-phrases are in a chain that links a +WH CP spec position and an A-position.

Reconsider the English multiple wh-construction (4), reproduced here as (11):

(11) $[_{CP} \, SM_x \, who_y \, C \, [_{IP} \, t_y \, saw \, what_x \,]]$

Recall that the Wh-Criterion (5) is stated on chains and therefore does not require the contentive wh-phrase to be in a spec-head relation with the

+WH C. As we saw, it would be satisfied by the English structure (6a), or the Hungarian (7a), reproduced here as (12a,b), where the wh-phrase remains in situ but forms a chain with an empty operator in spec-CP:

(12) a. *I wonder SM_x C Mary saw who_x
     b. *SM_x Ki_y t_y hozott mit_x
        who-nom brought what-acc
        'Who brought what'

Instead of excluding these under the assumption that the relevant features (of the +WH head and the wh-phrase, respectively) are strong, I now assume that these are ruled out by the Transparency principle in (10): the contentive *who* is not in the highest possible position in its chain. (For a much more detailed discussion of negation in terms of expletive-associate chains and the Transparency principle see Haegeman, forthcoming.)

The formation of the wh-chain in (11) is forced by the second clause (5b) of the Wh-Criterion, which requires that every wh-phrase must be chain-related to the spec of a +WH head. This is in accordance with Greed: the chain on the contentive α is formed to satisfy α's own requirement. The first clause (5a) of the Wh-Criterion, a requirement of the +WH head, plays no role in this account—as expected, given Greed. In fact, bringing together the two principles in (5) as the Wh-Criterion may well be spurious, since we can attribute the requirement in (5a) to a different and more general consideration. A +WH head is naturally thought of as marking the scope of the associated wh-phrase. (I assume that this scope-marking function is regularly transferred to the spec of the +WH head.) Thus if no wh-phrase is associated with a +WH head, then scope-marking will be vacuous. We can take this to be excluded by an appropriately extended version of the principle ruling out vacuous quantification.

A further advantage of Transparency has to do with the copy theory of movement/reconstruction (see chapter 5 for discussion). If movement leaves copies in trace positions, or in our terms if all chain members c-commanded by the contentive element are copies of the contentive, then it must be the case that only the highest member of such a set of copies (i.e., the contentive itself) is visible for SPELLOUT. Under a Procrastinate-inspired approach this is quite surprising: the contentive is in the lowest position of its chain, unless forced higher, but it is phonologically represented in its highest position. On the other hand, under the reasoning of the previous paragraph the fact that the SPELLOUT position of the contentive is the highest is as expected: the grammar is designed in such a way that where possible PF makes the (L)LF chain relations explicit. Hence the default position of the contentive is the highest in its chain and so is its SPELLOUT position.

To summarize this section: Procrastinate is problematic for several reasons. Most importantly, it appears to be incompatible with Greed and it predicts that in the default case LF and PF are maximally dissimilar. The economy problems with Earliness, on the other hand, can be resolved in terms of the representational principle of Transparency. Under the copy theory of movement, Transparency has the further advantage of making the parallel between the default (L)LF and default SPELLOUT positions expected.

4.4 "LF Movement" from A′-Positions

Let us turn to the question of contentives that occur in an A′-position that does not correspond to their scope—in standard terminology, the question of LF movement from A′-position. As we shall see, the present approach makes it possible to find a resolution to this recalcitrant problem.

Huang (1982) and Lasnik and Saito (1984) provided evidence from Chinese, Japanese, and Polish against a universal prohibition of LF movement from A′-positions. For example, on the assumption that the ECP forces the presence of an intermediate empty category between the adjunct wh-phrase and its scope marker in (13), the example must involve LF movement from A′-position (cf. Lasnik and Saito 1984, 1992).

(13) Bill-wa [John-ga naze$_x$ kubi-ni natta tte e$_x$] itta no SM$_x$
      Bill-top John-nom why   was fired   C   said Q
      'Why did Bill say that John was fired'

A similar point can be made on the basis of the so-called partial Wh-movement construction that occurs in a number of languages, including German, Romani (McDaniel 1989) and Hungarian. (14) is a Hungarian example.

(14) Mit mondott Mari hogy ki   ment el   tegnap?
      what said   M   that who went away yesterday
      'Who did Mary say left yesterday'

Here a default scope-marking wh-element is in the spec of the +WH C and the contentive wh-phrase is in a lower spec position. I assume that in some languages the scope-marking wh-phrase need not be overt. In other words, I assume that (14) is essentially the same construction as the Polish example in (15) discussed by Lasnik and Saito, which shows the contentive wh-phrase in an intermediate spec-CP but no overt expletive wh-element in the spec of the +WH C:

(15) Maria mysli, ze co   Janek kupil?
     M   thinks   what J   bought
     'What does Mary think that John bought'

If structures with and without overt scope markers are analyzed as instantiating the same construction, then partial Wh-movement (i.e., a wh-phrase in an A'-position that does not correspond to its scope) turns out to be quite frequent.

Consider, then, the German examples (16) and (17) (from McDaniel 1989):

(16) Wer glaubt t [mit wem   Jacob t gesprochen hat]
     Who believes   with whom Jacob   talked   has
     'Who believes that Jacob has talked to whom'

(17) Was glaubt Hans [mit wem   Jacob jetzt spricht t]
     What believes Hans   with whom Jacob now talks
     'With whom does Hans believe that Jacob is now talking'

In both (16) and (17) the wh-phrase in the -WH spec-CP of the embedded clause takes matrix scope. As the glosses show, both (16) and (17) are direct questions, (16) a multiple direct question. Example (16), which we might call a partial multiple Wh-movement construction, is apparently acceptable only in certain dialects of German. Example (17) exhibits partial Wh-movement, where the default wh-word *was* serves as a scope marker for the wh phrase in the WH spec CP of a lower clause.

Both partial and partial multiple wh-constructions are rather problematic for an analysis of English Wh-movement that makes use of a prohibition against LF-movement from A'-positions. Within the standard framework, the obvious analyses of (14), (15), (16), and (17) would have to involve just such movement, of the wh-phrase in -WH spec-CP to its scope position. But this means that the prohibition against LF movement from A'-position would have to be parametrized: it holds in English but not in German, Hungarian, or Polish, among others. Such a parameter seems theoretically undesirable since it is incompatible with the restriction of parameters to (some subpart of) the lexicon. LF-movement is not a property of any lexical item, hence we do not expect its characteristics to vary from language to language.

Furthermore, there is strong empirical evidence against such an approach. Overt scope relations between elements in A'-positions seem to be generally fixed in all languages (E-Kiss 1984; Williams 1986; Epstein 1991). For example, in (18) the overt A'-position of the topicalized quantificational element, *every problem*, must correspond to its scope position. Similarly, in the multiple wh-construction (19), the scope of the wh-phrases in A'-position is fixed; only that of the wh-in-situ is ambiguous:

(18) Somebody thinks that every problem$_x$ Mary solved t$_x$

(19) Who$_x$ t$_x$ wondered where$_y$ we bought what t$_y$

Thus the prohibition against LF movement from A'-position would have to be suspended in German, Hungarian, and so on, only in the case of the partial (and in some dialects in the partial multiple) wh-construction.

McDaniel suggests that the parameter that underlies the difference between English and German here has to do with the point of application of the absorption rule of Higginbotham and May (1981), which can apply at S-structure in German (to wh-phrases that are not necessarily in the same spec-CP) but only at LF in English. S-structure absorption in German creates a chain between the S-structure A'-position of the wh-phrase and its scope position. Hence this chain captures an S-structure relation, and no LF chain is initiated here from an A'-position. Although such an approach avoids the empirical problems of the previous paragraph, the suggested parameter remains undesirable: it is no more lexical than a parametrized prohibition on LF movement from A'-position. It also involves an otherwise unmotivated extension of the absorption rule to nonlocal relations. Furthermore, the account crucially involves S-structure and thus could not be adopted in a minimalist theory.

In terms of the present theory, the question of when or whether "LF movement" from A'-position is permitted translates into the question of when or whether an expletive-contentive chain can be formed in cases where the contentive element is in an A'-position (more precisely, in a potential scope-position; cf. Rizzi 1991.) For most cases Transparency and spec-head licensing provide the solution. Consider (20) and (21b), where the contentive wh-phrase is in an intermediate A'-position.

(20) *John wondered SM$_x$ C Mary thought what$_x$ you saw t$_x$

(21) a.   John wondered SM_x who$_y$ t_y thought that Mary saw what$_x$
     b. *John wondered SM_x who$_y$ t_y thought what$_x$ Mary saw t_x

The structure in (20) meets the chain conditions in the Wh-Criterion in (5)
and is ruled out for two other reasons. First, the interrogative wh-phrase
is in a spec position (of a -WH C) where it is not licensed. Second, it is not
in its highest licensed position (the spec of the matrix +WH C), hence it is
also ruled out by Transparency. (21b) is ruled out only by the former of
these two considerations. Again, both (21a) and (21b) meet the conditions
that (5) takes together as the Wh-Criterion, but in (21b) the interrogative
wh-phrase is in a spec position (of a -WH C) where it is not licensed. The
wh-phrase in the intermediate A′-position in (21b) is not ruled out by
Transparency. It would not be licensed in the higher spec-(+WH)CP.
This position contains another wh-phrase and English allows only a single
wh-contentive associated with one +WH head.

As for partial Wh-movement structures, our assumption must be that
the wh-phrase moves to the highest position where it is licensed in accordance with Transparency. Suppose, then, that some feature of the intermediate head licenses a wh-contentive in these constructions. We could
assume that the relevant licensing feature in many (perhaps all?) such
cases has to do with focusing, as Rita Manzini (personal communication)
and a reviewer also noted. Recall that I attribute the lack of "Wh-movement" in Japanese-type languages to the fact that wh-contentives are not
licensed in the spec-CP position. Hence these languages cannot have
constructions that parallel (14)–(17) with respect to the position of the
contentive wh-phrase.

Topicalization can be treated along similar lines. Consider (22). Within
the standard framework this corresponds to a case of improper LF
movement from A′-position, where the topicalized quantifier phrase *every
problem* would further "topicalize" at LF, that is, move into a higher A′-
position:

(22) *SM_x Somebody thinks that every problem$_x$ Mary solved t_x

But Transparency excludes (22). If Topicalization involves no spec-head
relation, then the contentive will be vacuously licensed in all positions of
the chain; hence by Transparency it must be in the matrix clause in (22). If
Topicalization must be licensed in a spec-head configuration, then we can
assume that a head with the appropriate "topic" feature always licenses a
contentive. Again, therefore, the lexical category must be in the highest
position of its chain, excluding (22).

It remains to account for the lack of chains where the contentive that is not the head of its chain is in the spec of a +WH C—in other words, the lack of LF movement from the spec of a +WH head.

(23) a. *SM_x Who_y +WH t_y wondered SM_z $where_x$ +WH we bought $what_z$ t_x

b. SM_x Who_y +WH t_y wondered $what_z$ +WH we bought t_z $where_x$

As a string, (23a) can of course have grammatical structures, but the interpretation indicated is impossible. This corresponds to the case where in terms of the standard framework *where* would move at LF from the embedded CP to the matrix one, and *what* from in-situ position to the embedded CP. One possibility might be to exclude this configuration, using the principle of "minimize the number of chains," suggested in Chomsky 1993. Suppose that the expletive-associate and the associate-trace sections of a chain count as two separate chains for this principle. Then (23a) will contain two wh-chains associated with *where*. Depending on which subchain *where* is taken to belong to, we have either [SM,where] and [t] or [SM] and [where,t]. If *where* stayed in situ and *what* occupied the embedded CP overtly, then there would be only one chain for *where*, as in (23b). This structure must then be preferred over (23a). This solution does not presuppose the representational view; it can be restated in the derivational framework in terms of the assumption that overt and covert subparts of a chain count as distinct chains.

The stipulation that the two parts of the chain in fact form separate chains appears to lack independent evidence. Furthermore, the solution is problematic since it would appear to also exclude structures in which a covert A'-chain has a root that is the head of an overt A-chain: "Who believed what to have been eaten t," for example. Within the radical minimalist framework, on the other hand, the impossibility of this structure can be attributed to an independently necessary condition. As noted in the previous section, a +WH head is naturally considered as marking the scope of the wh-phrase associated with it, a function that it regularly transfers to its spec node(s). This means that in a structure like (23) there are two scope markers associated with *where*: SM in the matrix CP and *where* itself. The impossibility of (23a) thus can be attributed to the conflict created by double scope-marking. Chain-externally, multiple scope-marking will be excluded as a special case of the principle ruling out vacuous quantification, itself a consequence of FI. Chain-internally, we can derive the restriction by generalizing the assumption that a chain can contain only a single contentive to scope markers. An A'-chain is the abstract representation of a contentive with scope, and therefore cannot contain more than one of these elements.

Let us look briefly at some other accounts of the restriction on contentives in A'-positions. Rizzi (1991), essentially in the spirit of the approach in Lasnik and Saito 1984, proposed to allow the Wh-Criterion to apply both at LF and at S-structure. The second requirement of this principle, that all wh-phrases must be in a spec-head relation with a +WH head, entails that S-structures like (20) and (21b) are ruled out. This proposal, using S-structure conditions, would not only be incompatible with the minimalist approach (radical or not), but is also problematic for independent reasons.

First, in order to allow wh-in-situ, Rizzi has to restrict the S-structure application of the Wh-criterion to wh-operators, where wh-operators are wh-phrases in A'-positions. As he notes, this characterization of wh-operators cannot hold at the LF of the standard Principles and Parameters theory, where "it is superseded by a stronger principle according to which all elements endowed with intrinsic quantificational force are operators ... and must be moved to an appropriate scope position" (Rizzi 1991, 22n.5). But it is dubious to make the semantic concept of operator relevant at S-structure, particularly if this concept is different from the corresponding LF notion.

Partial multiple wh-constructions exemplified in (16) (reproduced here as (24)) create another problem for Rizzi's theory.

(24) Wer glaubt t [mit wem   Jacob t gesprochen hat]
     Who believes with whom Jacob talked   has
     'Who believes that Jacob has talked to whom'

Rizzi suggests that partial wh movement examples like (17) (also reproduced here as (25)) can be made compatible with the S-structure Wh-Criterion if this "is interpreted as applying on the head of the A'-chain of the wh-operator" (p. 22).

(25) Was glaubt Hans [mit wem   Jacob jetzt spricht t]
     What believes Hans with whom Jacob now talks
     'With whom does Hans believe that Jacob is now talking'

Thus he appears to assume with McDaniel that in these examples an S-structure chain is created between the wh-phrase and its scope-marker. Suppose we extend this approach to the partial multiple wh-construction and assume again that an S-structure chain links the two wh-phrases. Then the question that remains outstanding is why the Wh-Criterion cannot be similarly satisfied in the English equivalent of (16)/(24), why such an S-structure chain cannot be created in English. As I noted above, a parameter that allows such a chain to be constructed in German but not in English is quite undesirable.

Another serious drawback of Rizzi's approach is that the result of applying the Wh-Criterion at S-structure does not seem general enough. It does not exclude structures like (23) where the Wh-Criterion is satisfied, although not by the same relationships, both at S-structure and at LF. As we have seen, the prohibition against LF movement from A'-position is relevant also to non-wh categories: for example, the topicalized element in (22) cannot take matrix scope, either.

Epstein (1991) proposed to rule out LF movement from A'-position with the help of Chomsky's economy principle that requires that the length of derivations be minimized. He assumed that LF movement is not constrained by Subjacency. Given this assumption, direct LF movement from the in-situ position to the +WH spec-CP in (20) and (21b) (reproduced as (26) and (27))involves only one step, while S-structure movement to the intermediate position results together with further LF raising minimally in a two-step derivation. The account is the same for (22) and (23), reproduced as (28):

(26) *John wondered SM_x C Mary thought $what_x$ you saw t_x

(27) a. John wondered SM_x who_y t_y thought that Mary saw $what_x$
      b. *John wondered SM_x who_y t_y thought $what_x$ Mary saw t_x

(28) a. *SM_x Who_y t_y wondered SM_z $where_x$ we bought $what_z$ t_x
      b. *SM_x Somebody thinks that every $problem_x$ Mary solved t_x

But as I have argued in chapter 2, Subjacency does constrain the wh-relations that the LF movement of standard Principles and Parameters theory captures. Thus in general, the S-structure raising to an intermediate position will not result in a longer derivation. Furthermore, as noted in chapter 1, minimizing the number of derivational steps conflicts with minimizing the length of these steps. As we saw, an account in terms of minimizing the number of chains also seems quite dubious.

The account of (26) and (27) can be restated in terms of Procrastinate and the assumption that -WH C does not force overt movement. Similarly, (28b) can be excluded by taking "topic" features to be invariably strong; the quantified topic will then have to be in the matrix clause. The account of (28a) in terms of the principle excluding vacuous scope-marking does not seem to be easily restatable in the standard derivational framework, however, since it is based on the existence of a level like LLF where the scope marker and the wh-phrase in its PF position are simultaneously present. Neither PF nor LF satisfies this description.

4.5   QR and Antecedent-Contained Ellipsis

Let us also consider the status of Quantifier raising (QR) in the radically minimalist theory. One crucial question here is whether the relation standardly expressed by QR exhibits the usual cluster of movement properties. Since it is not clear a priori what positions are involved, one cannot tell if the MTC is respected. Thus, under the standard adjunction analysis, QR obeys the MTC, but under the assumptions of Williams 1986, where the relevant relationship is taken to be between the quantified phrase and some node that contains it, the MTC may or may not be observed (depending on whether this node can ever be an argument in a theta position). May (1985) has argued that QR is constrained by the ECP, but Williams 1986 and Lasnik and Saito 1992 raise problems for his analysis.

Since the relation expressed by QR is generally clause-bound, Subjacency effects cannot appear. Reinhart (1991) disagreed with this generalization. Her argument is based on certain apparently elliptic conjunctions like (29). She argues that QR must apply in these to provide the appropriate interpretation:

(29) No one kissed his mother except Felix

(30) "No one except Felix kissed his mother"

(31) "No one kissed his mother and/except Felix kissed his mother"

(32) The critics liked your book and the public too

(33) More people love Mozart than Bach

Analysing (29) as a standard ellipsis structure would incorrectly yield the contradictory (31). Reinhart takes QR to raise the correlate *no one* to adjoin to the 'remnant' *except Felix* of the apparent ellipsis. QR thus allows these two categories to combine as in (30) to provide the appropriate meaning. Reinhart argues that Bare Argument Ellipsis, as in (32), and Comparative Ellipsis, as in (33), should be analysed in a similar fashion.

She then takes examples like (34)–(36), where the 'remnant' follows some apparently matrix clause material, to demonstrate that QR is not clause-bound:

(34) Lucie will admit that she stole the diamonds if you press her but not the car

(35) Lucie did not admit that she stole anything, when we pressed her, except the little red book

(36) More people said they will vote for Bush, in the last poll, than for Dukakis

But it is not clear if these examples are really grammatical. Perhaps the 'remnant' is still associated with the embedded clause here and there is some 'stylistic' reordering between the 'remnant' and the interpolated clause, creating a degree of acceptability. This view is reinforced by the observation that if QR really raised the correlate higher than the matrix clause, we would expect this phrase to be able to have scope over all quantificational elements in the structure. But scope over the matrix clause is not possible. (37a) cannot have the interpretation (37c). It can only be understood as in (37b), with matrix *someone* retaining scope over "everything (except the car)."

(37) a. Someone will admit that we stole everything if you insist, except the car
     b. "Someone will admit that everything except the car we stole, if you insist"
     c. "For everything except the car, someone will admit that we stole it, if you insist"

It appears then that the acceptability of the examples in (37) cannot be due to QR having applied clause-externally. Rather it seems that the interpolated clauses "if you insist" and so on do not reliably indicate that the 'remnant' is associated with the higher clause. The hypothesis that interpolated clauses are subject to some stylistic reordering is reinforced by (38). Here the matrix category "to our friends" that follows the embedded clause is less easily taken to be interpolated material subject to such reordering. Accordingly, (38) seems still less acceptable than the examples in (34), (35) and (36).

(38) John admitted that Mary stole everything to our old friends except the diamonds

(Irrelevantly, (34)–(36) and (38) seem acceptable also with the *except*-clause taken as an afterthought, a construal that comes with the contradictory interpretation.) Thus the evidence Reinhart provides does not seriously challenge the view that in the general case (and in particular with quantifiers like *every*) QR is clause-bound, unlike standard chain/movement relations. All in all, the evidence that the QR relation is of the same kind as the one standardly expressed by Move α is not very strong.

A different issue is whether scope relations must be disambiguated at (L)LF. This is not necessarily the case; in theory, nontrivial principles applied to syntactic representations could explicate scope (see Aoun and Li 1989 for such a theory). If scope must be disambiguated at (L)LF, as I shall tentatively assume (cf. Hornstein and Weinberg 1990, or more recently Stowell and Beghelli 1994), then we could keep to the program of reducing scope relations to c/m-command relations holding between scope markers (cf. Williams 1986). As just noted, I take the relation between the scope marker and the surface position of the quantified expression not to be a chain relation, but the approach in terms of scope markers is compatible also with the opposite view. Thus phenomena related to QR appear in general to raise no problem of principle for the LLF approach.

Fiengo and May's (1990) evidence for QR, on the other hand, does challenge the radical minimalist framework, in which no deplacement of lexical material can take place in syntax. They appear to show that QR must actually change the position of certain categories before the level where binding theory applies, that is, before the syntactic interface level. Their argument is based on antecedent-contained VP-deletion structures like (39):

(39) a. John {suspected [everyone that Mary did]}

b. [Everyone that Mary did] John {suspected t}

The (curly-bracketed) antecedent of the anaphoric VP in (39a) contains the anaphoric VP. A strict identity requirement between antecedent and elided VP would thus result in infinite regress. Substituting the antecedent "suspected everyone that Mary did" creates each time another VP-elision context with the same antecedent. Thus apparently no appropriate identical antecedent can be found before QR applies, as in (39b). (See also May 1985; Larson and May 1990 for the assumption that QR must precede VP-interpretation.) Fiengo and May point out further that the binding theory must operate on structures where the elided VP is present. If the binding theory holds at LF, then it follows from these ordering requirements that QR must precede LF, in other words that there is a syntactic rule of QR.

Examples like (40) and (41) from Fiengo and May convincingly show that the elided VP must be present at the level where binding theory applies, the level of (L)LF in minimalist frameworks.

(40) a. *Mary introduced him_x to [everyone that he_x did]
      b. [Everyone that he_x {introduced him_x to e}] Mary {introduced him_x to e}

(41) a. Mary introduced herself to [everyone that Betsy did]
      b. [Everyone that $Betsy_x$ {introduced $herself_x$ to e}] $Mary_y$ {introduced $herself_y$ to e}

In (40) the two pronouns are disjoint in reference, a regular principle B effect where the elided VP is present, but apparently unexplainable in terms of the S-structure configuration of (40a). (41a) has a sloppy reading, but binding of the anaphor to the embedded subject *Betsy* is again not possible in the absence of the elided VP. Assume then that the elided VP is present at LF. I shall question the other half of the argument, that QR, a rule that deplaces lexical material, must precede the level where this VP is expressed.

Fiengo and May introduce the concept of "vehicle change" to explain the lack of principle C violation in examples like (42) and (43):

(42) a. Mary introduced $John_x$ to everyone that he_x wanted her to
      b. Mary introduced $John_x$ to everyone that he_x wanted her to introduce him_x to

(43) a. Mary loves $John_x$ and he_x thinks that Betsy does too
      b. Mary loves $John_x$ and he_x thinks that Betsy loves him_x too

Coreference between *John* and *he* is possible in both (42a) and (43a); the interpretations indicated under (42b) and (43b) are possible. (42b) and (43b) do not exhibit complete identity between the elided/interpreted VP and its antecedent: the proper name *John* has been substituted by an appropriate pronoun in the anaphoric VP. Fiengo and May argue that such substitutions of a "pronominal correlate" are legitimate instances of what they call vehicle change and make the observed interpretation possible. Once the proper name is substituted by its pronominal correlate, principle C is not violated here.

But the concept of vehicle change, well motivated by examples like (42) and (43), can also be used to avoid the problem of infinite regress with the null VP in all of these antecedent-contained deletion structures without invoking QR. Suppose that the VP-interpretation can use a variable as a correlate of the category that undergoes QR in Fiengo and May's analysis. The LF structure of (39) will be then (44), where t is the variable correlate of the square-bracketed NP:

(44) John {suspected [everyone that Mary did {suspect t}]}

No displacing of lexical material by QR is necessary then to resolve the problem of regress in VP-reconstruction.

Wyngaerd and Zwart (1991), who proposed essentially the same solution independently, assume that the same vehicle change to a variable correlate is instantiated also in cases like (45):

(45) a. Dulles suspected Philby, who Angleton did {suspect t} too
     b. John kissed Mary, but I wonder who Harry did {kiss t}

More recently, Fiengo and May (1994) agreed with the analyses in (45), where a proper name has a variable correlate, but rejected the similar vehicle-change approach for the basic antecedent-contained ellipsis case in (44). (I will argue below that there is some reason to believe that the situation is exactly the opposite: variables can substitute for quantificational expressions, but not for names, under vehicle change.) They claim in a footnote that reconstruction of the VP in cases like (44) cannot be a result of vehicle change of the relative clause: "vehicle change is sensitive only to the full class of arguments as defined by the nominal typology, thus it is applicable to variables but not to the operators that bind them" (Fiengo and May 1994, 238n.2). But this remark appears only to repeat the assumption at issue. (The footnote refers also to their chapter 5, but the general characterization of vehicle change given there is inconsistent with this assumption: "in a reconstruction a nominal can take any syntactic form so long as its indexical structure (type and value) is unchanged" (Fiengo and May 1994, 218). They state in that chapter that the vehicle change from a name to a variable is made possible by the fact that these belong to the same cell of the standard nominal typology. But part of this issue is precisely whether the typology is the correct one. If quantified phrases are in situ where the binding theory applies, as I claim, then they must fall under the same cell of the nominal typology as names in those respects that are relevant for the binding theory. In other respects, quantified phrases might fall together with variables but not with names; see below.)

The interaction of scope facts with principle C of the binding theory strongly reinforces the conclusion that no pre-(L)LF QR is involved in antecedent-contained ellipsis.

(46) a. *He$_x$ suspected [everyone John$_x$ could]
     b. *He$_x$ met [everyone John$_x$ wanted to]

Coreference between *he* and *John* is prohibited in (46), showing that no QR that pied piped the relative clause could have applied before the interface level where the binding theory holds. Notice that pied piping of the relative is necessary in Fiengo and May's account to ensure that the elided VP is not contained in its antecedent, where reconstruction applies.

In order to account for the ungrammaticality of these examples, Fiengo and May (1990) propose that QR adjoins the bracketed NP not to IP but to the VP. The LF structure of (46) would then be (47):

(47) He$_x$ [$_{VP}$ [everyone John$_x$ could//wanted to] [$_{VP}$ met t]]

The principle C configuration at the post-QR level is thus preserved, excluding coreference appropriately. But this does not solve the problem in general, since *everyone* can have higher scope than the subject, as in (48), and under this construal disjointness still obtains (*someone* = someone other than *John*).

(48) Someone met everyone that John could//wanted to

Note that an analysis like (49) cannot help. Here only the quantifier *everyone* has IP-scope, whereas the rest of the QP is adjoined to VP, but this does not correspond to the interpretation of the sentence.

(49) Everyone$_x$ Someone [$_{VP}$ x [that John did//wanted to] [$_{VP}$ met t]]

Fiengo and May 1994 contains a different attempt at resolving this difficulty for their approach. They propose essentially that the binding theory applies to an index at every level where all occurrences of the index appear. Thus when some occurrence of an index is in an elided VP, then the binding theory can only apply at LF, where the elided structure is reconstructed. But (46) contains no occurrences of the index x in the elided structure, so binding theory can already apply at S-structure where all occurences of this index are present, excluding the structure. The suggestion is incompatible with the minimalist restriction of representational

constraints to the interface levels. Furthermore, it is easy to show that this
proposal does not help either to circumvent the evidence from principle C
against the QR approach. The immediate prediction that an occurrence of
the relevant index in the elided VP will nullify the principle C violation is
clearly incorrect:

(50) *He$_x$ thought he$_x$ suspected everyone Bill$_x$ did {thought he$_x$
      suspected}

Coreference in (50) does not become possible if the elided VP is taken to
correspond to the matrix VP, as indicated, rather than to the embedded
one. But on Fiengo and May's account, in (50) principle C should not
apply at S-structure. Their solution thus incorrectly makes coreference
legitimate in this sentence.

   Fiengo and May also find a contrast between (51) and (52):

(51) Mary introduced him$_x$ to everyone that John$_x$ wanted her to

(52) Mary introduced him$_x$ to everyone that John$_x$ wanted her to
      introduce him$_x$ to

They claim that the indicated coreference is worse in (52) than in (51), and
use this as a basis of an argument for the post-QR application of principle
C. However, it is not clear if the coreference contrast between (51) and
(52) is significant. Furthermore, even if there were a genuine contrast,
Fiengo and May's account (in terms of S-structure versus LF application
of principle C, conditioned by the presence of all occurrences of the
relevant index) would conflict with the clear datum in (50).

   Thus QR not only does not need to precede VP-interpretation, there is
evidence that it should not do so. Even though the elided VP must be
present at (L)LF, no displacement operation like QR should precede this
level.

   Although Fiengo and May (1994) do not discuss the vehicle-change
solution to antecedent-contained ellipsis directly (beyond the remark
quoted above), they give several arguments against dispensing with QR in
the explanation of antecedent-contained ellipsis. Apart from the argument
involving principle C, already discussed, these originate in Larson and
May 1990 and are based on cases where reconstruction possibilities
appear to be a function of the scope of quantification involved.

   Larson and May and Fiengo and May note that (53a) is ambiguous
between the interpretations in (53b) and (53c):

(53) a. John wants to visit [every city you do]
   b. John wants to visit every city you visit
   c. John wants to visit every city you want to visit

They note that the interpretation in (53b) is possible with both matrix and embedded scope of the bracketed QP, while the "broad" reconstruction in (53c) is only possible with the bracketed QP taking matrix scope. Although the effect is not very strong, it seems real. The correlation is explained by the QR account: with narrow scope of the QP and broad reconstruction the elided VP is still inside its antecedent; the structure would still lead to infinite regress in reconstruction. But the radical minimalist approach using vehicle change can also rule out the missing interpretation on the assumption that scope is disambiguated at LLF. If there is a scope marker associated with the QP in (53), then on the narrow-scope broad-reconstruction reading the structure will be (54):

(54) John {wants SM to visit [every city you {want SM to visit t}]}

The scope marker indicating the scope of the bracketed QP will be reconstructed in the elided VP, in violation of the prohibition against vacuous scope-marking, (see the previous section for this principle). No such extra scope marker will appear on the narrow-scope narrow-reconstruction (55a) or the broad-scope broad-reconstruction (55b) readings:

(55) a. John wants SM {to visit every city you visit}
   b. SM John {wants to visit every city you want to visit}

   Their argument from scope relations in (56) translates similarly into a framework without movement:

(56) Dulles believed [everyone that Hoover did] to be a spy

In (56) the elided VP again must be understood as taking the matrix VP as its antecedent. This forces matrix scope for the bracketed QP. In Fiengo and May's terms this is to avoid antecedent containment at the point where reconstruction applies. In my terms this is to avoid vacuous scope-marking as in (57):

(57) Dulles {believed SM everyone that Hoover {believed SM t to be a spy} to be a spy}

   Larson and May and Fiengo and May also argue that QR is operative in the account of antecedent-contained ellipsis based on the ungrammaticality of structures like (58), in contrast to the much milder unacceptability of (56).

(58) *Dulles believed [everyone that Hoover did] is a spy

On the assumption that QR cannot raise a QP from a tensed clause, the ungrammaticality of (58) and the acceptability of (56) follows on their account. In (58), where the QP cannot be raised from the embedded clause, the antecedent will continue to include the elided VP after QR. In contrast, in (56) the QP can raise out of the matrix VP, which therefore will cease to contain the anaphoric VP, making reconstruction possible. Again the movement operation can be dispensed with, since this account can also be exchanged for one in terms of scope markers. If a tensed subject QP cannot have clause-external scope then the prohibition of vacuous scope-marking will exclude also structures like (58) in the same way it excluded the previous cases in (54) and (57). There are, however, at least two reasons why the correlation between quantifier scope and reconstruction here seems dubious.

First, as Lasnik (1993) points out, the assumption that the quantifier in (58) cannot have matrix scope contradicts the strongly worded position of May (1988), who observes that both (59) and (60) exhibit the possibility of the universal quantifier taking scope over the wh-phrase:

(59) Who do you think everyone saw at the rally

(60) What did everyone buy for Max

Second, even if universal quantifiers could not take matrix scope from a tensed clause, wh-phrases in situ uncontroversially can. They create only mild unacceptability in unconnected (in the sense of Kayne 1983) subject positions:

(61) Who said (that) who brought this present

But even though the wh-phrase in tensed subject position can take matrix scope with only mild unacceptability, antecedent-contained ellipsis internal to it remains completely impossible:

(62) *Who believed (that) which man that Hoover did is a spy

Thus no correlation between the scope of the containing QP and the possibility of antecedent-contained ellipsis appears to hold in this configuration.

In fact the ungrammaticality of (58) and (62) is reminiscent of the well-known cases of Pesetsky's "surprising" asymmetries (cf. Browning 1987; Frampton 1990, forthcoming; Cinque 1991). Take the reconstructed structure of (58):

(63) *Dulles {believed [everyone that Hoover {believed t is a spy}] is a spy}

The subject trace in the elided VP, the correspondent under vehicle change of the containing QP, is in a position that creates ungrammaticality in other constructions. These include Wh-movement across islands and various empty operator constructions, as exemplified by adjectival complements and parasitic gaps:

(64) *John is easy to believe t is a spy

(65) *Who did you hire although you believed t was a spy

Like the less strong violation in the antecedent-contained ECM case (56), the ECM cases with the other surprising asymmetry constructions show weaker violations:

(66) ??John is easy to believe t to be a spy

(67) ??Who did you hire although you believed t to be a spy

In sum, Fiengo and May provide no reasons to believe that an account of antecedent-contained ellipsis in terms of vehicle change that dispenses with the movement rule of QR is incorrect. Principle C effects provide clear evidence that antecedent-contained ellipsis should not be treated in terms of QR. The correlations with quantifier scope exhibited by this construction can be treated in the nonderivational framework in terms of the prohibition against vacuous scope-marking. I have also questioned the validity of some of these correlations. (For additional arguments against post-QR reconstruction and a different analysis see Lappin 1992, forthcoming.)

Let me finally discuss briefly the analysis of antecedent-contained ellipsis given recently by Lasnik (1993) and Hornstein (1994). They independently provide essentially the same alternative explanation of the contrast between (56) and (58), reproduced here as (68) and (69):

(68)   Dulles believed [everyone that Hoover did] to be a spy

(69) *Dulles believed [everyone that Hoover did] is a spy

Both Hornstein and Lasnik assume with Fiengo and May, and contrary to the vehicle-change account defended here, that at the level where reconstruction operates the anaphoric VP of antecedent-contained ellipsis must be external to its antecedent. They attribute the contrast between (68) and (69) to the assumption that in the ECM construction, covert object shift will move out the bracketed phrase into the matrix clause, while in the tensed clause the bracketed subject will remain internal to the embedded clause and therefore internal to the matrix VP. Hence by LF the elided VP will be external to its antecedent in the ECM case (68) but not in the tensed subject case (69).

Lasnik's additional evidence for this account is based on cases of antecedent-contained ellipsis internal to nonrestrictive relatives that are in nonstructurally Case-marked positions:

(70) *Mary {stood near [Susan, who Emily did as well]}

(71) *John {showed the teacher [Susan, who Mary did too]}

The ungrammaticality of these examples follows immediately under Lasnik's assumptions if the nonrestrictive relative forms a constituent with its head: since raising to spec-Agr is not available in these examples, the antecedent will contain the elided VP at LF.

Examples like (70) and (71) are grammatical, however, with restrictive relatives:

(72) Mary {stood near [everyone Emily did]}

(73) John {showed the teacher [everyone Mary did]}

To account for similar apparent antecedent-contained ellipsis cases where object shift is impossible, Hornstein assumes that the category containing the elided VP is generated as an adjunct, outside the antecedent VP. There are two immediate strong reasons to reject this hypothesis. Given antecedent-contained ellipsis, for example, in double-object constructions like (73) or *about*-PPs, such subcategorized elements would have to be treated as VP-external adjuncts, as Hornstein notes. But even this radical assumption will not help, since the reconstructed VPs will now lack the crucial variable, leading to vacuous quantification by the relative operator. Note also that the proposal would not account for the contrast between the restrictive and the nonrestrictive relative cases either.

Lasnik makes a different proposal. He claims that the restrictive and the nonrestrictive structures contrast because restrictives but not nonrestrictives can extrapose:

(74) A man arrived who was wearing a red hat

(75) *John arrived who was wearing a red hat

Thus, resurrecting in part and in a modified form Baltin's (1987) analysis, he proposes that the grammaticality of antecedent-contained ellipsis in nonrestrictive relatives that are in nonstructurally Case-marked positions (i.e., (72) and (73)) is due to extraposition. Examples (72) and (73) can have the structures in (76) and (77), respectively. Extraposition (of the bracketed relative clause) ensures the presence of an antecedent for the elided VP that does not contain it. (Lasnik suggests that under the copy theory of movement the copy of the quantifier can act as a trace.)

(76) Mary {stood near everyone} (Emily {stood near everyone })

(77) John {showed the teacher everyone} (Mary {showed the teacher everyone})

Lasnik assumes further that the extraposition rule involved here is covert, operating in the LF component. This is necessary given the fact that the nonrestrictive relatives in (72) and (73) can occur with a null complementizer (as exemplified), something that overtly extraposed clauses cannot do. If the prohibition against the null complementizer holds at PF, then LF extraposition will of course not violate it.

(78) I visited a man recently who/that/?*∅ John mentioned

Lasnik's account of antecedent-contained ellipsis, just like Fiengo and May's, is incompatible with the radical minimalist framework. This account also crucially assumes that covert movement of lexical material is necessary to resolve the configuration of antecedent containment. Both covert object shift and covert extraposition (just like Fiengo and May's covert QR) entail that at LF lexical material is in a position different from where it occurs at PF. Notice that while overt movement can be treated representationally simply as chain formation (i.e., linking of a category containing lexical material to other positions), covert movement could only be handled in a representational framework very unnaturally. In covert movement constructions, lexical material would appear at different positions at LF and at PF, necessitating movement or some equivalent.

On the assumption that the contrast between the ECM and the tensed subject case of antecedent-contained ellipsis in (68) and (69) is parallel to the other surprising asymmetry constructions, Lasnik's approach to (69) is problematic. As it is designed only to deal with the antecedent-contained ellipsis cases, it cannot be generalized in any obvious way to capture the whole range of relevant data.

Second, the covert extraposition rule that is crucially involved in the account of the various contrasts between restrictives and nonrestrictives is not only incompatible with the radically minimalist framework, but is also somewhat dubious for independent reasons. First, there are problems that may be of a technical nature concerning the copy of the quantified head of the relative in structures like (76) and (77): if this is present only at some level prior to LF, as Lasnik appears to assume, then either the identity constraints on reconstruction must be stated prior to LF, a serious problem in the minimalist approach, or some additional apparatus (QR, vehicle change, etc.) is necessary. Related problems arise concerning the trace of the extraposed clause: what is the status of its correspondent in the elided VP?

Third, the covert extraposition necessary in cases of broad reconstruction with tensed embedded clauses would need to move the extraposed element into the matrix clause, an operation extraposition is known not to be capable of:

(79) John believes Mary met everyone Bill does

Consider broad reconstruction in (79), which takes the matrix VP as the antecedent. This is perhaps not perfect, but clearly possible. (I agree here with the judgement of Fiengo and May contra Baltin and Hornstein. I assume that the contrast between tensed and infinitival embedded clauses on broad reconstruction is due to the tense-island constraint on the trace in the reconstructed VP that corresponds under vehicle change to the relative clause—another manifestation of the parallel between antecedent-contained ellipsis and the various surprising asymmetry constructions.) Under Lasnik's account this reading is accessible only if covert extraposition moves the relative clause into the matrix; otherwise it and therefore the elided VP will remain internal to its antecedent, the matrix VP. But extraposition cannot do this.

Let us reject, then, the covert extraposition rule, and return to the earlier solution in terms of vehicle change. We could integrate into this approach the object shift account of the contrasts between restrictive and nonrestrictive relatives with respect to antecedent-contained ellipsis in the following way. Suppose that vehicle change can only introduce a variable for quantified phrases, but not for proper names. This is natural in the LLF framework, where quantified phrases stay in situ, and therefore in some sense incorporate an occurrence of the variable they bind (cf. Williams 1986). Vehicle change cannot introduce variables for constants, however. This means that nonrestrictive relatives cannot resolve the infinite regress in reconstruction through vehicle change: they have to do so by object shift. Since neither vehicle change nor object shift is possible in (70) and (71), the antecedent-contained ellipsis is ill-formed here. Notice that in the radical minimalist framework this explanation would entail that objects are in spec-Agr in English (in standard terminology, that object shift is overt); see, for example, Johnson 1991, and Koizumi 1993 for arguments for this position.

4.6 Conclusion

I have considered in this chapter the question of where the contentive element appears in its chain. I argued that there is a default position: in the spirit of Earliness, this is the highest licensed position of the chain. I argued against taking the default position of the contentive to be the root position of the chain in the spirit of Procrastinate. Perhaps the most important reason for this is that Procrastinate predicts that (L)LF and PF are different in the default case and become similar only as a consequence of morphological accidents. I proposed a principle of Transparency that could resolve certain theoretical problems of the Earliness principle within the nonderivational LLF theory, and that had the further advantage of predicting the parallel between default LLF positions and SPELLOUT positions under the copy theory of movement. The LLF approach had the further advantage of being able to account for the prohibition against LF "movement" from A'-position in the multiple wh case also, using the independently motivated principle ruling out vacuous quantification. I also considered QR and noted that the evidence that this is a chain relation is weak. Finally I discussed antecedent-contained ellipsis and argued that given the independently necessary concept of vehicle change this construction does not need to and should not involve (covert) movement of any kind, either.

Chapter 5
Reconstruction and Partially Determined Full Interpretation

5.1 Introduction

The wh-in-situ constructions were taken in standard Principles and Parameters theory to motivate the postulation of an LF raising rule. I have argued that this analysis is well motivated in taking the relation between the wh-in-situ and its scope to be of the same type as the relations that Move α generally captures, and therefore this analysis is superior to the more recent interpretive approaches. But the process of Move α that displaces the lexical element is unnecessary to treat the wh-in-situ construction. That phenomenon can equally well be captured in terms of chains, a concept that in itself involves no assumption about the position of the lexical category it contains. Thus it is possible to keep to the minimal assumption, that there is no derivation during which the position of the lexical category could change.

There is different class of phenomena, the various so-called reconstruction effects, where again a lexical element appears to have to occur at LF in a position that is different from the one it occupies at PF. The term *reconstruction* refers to those cases in which, in contrast to wh-in-situ, the LF position of the lexical category is lower than its PF position. Since the evidence appears to show that the lexical element must be in this lower position at LF, it has generally been assumed that at this level a copy of the lexical element appears in the reconstructed position. The movement theory of reconstruction makes the further assumption that at LF only this copy appears; the lexical element in the overt position must delete.

The evidence shows, I argue in this chapter, that at (L)LF both the original and the copy of the contentive element must be present, and thus no deletion takes place (and therefore no movement, which involves deletion). Such a theory appears to be precluded by the principle of FI, which requires every element at LF to have an appropriate interpretation. Since no element can be ignored at LF, interpretively redundant elements cannot be present here. The contradiction is only apparent—recall that chains and not chain-members are the elements input to principles of interpretation. I have assumed throughout that FI is neutral with respect to the content of the elements interpretive principles operate on. Since chains are the relevant units for interpretation, the internal construction of these is not constrained by FI. Thus FI does not prevent the contentive category from being present in more than one position in the chain.

This approach in effect takes the position of the contentive to be indeterminate at LF. This means that the LF structures I propose will not differentiate the reconstructed from the nonreconstructed interpretations of a sentence. To express this ambiguity of the LF structures, I shall call the hypothesis the Partially Determined Full Interpretation (PDFI) approach. The PDFI approach is similar to the standard minimalist theory in assuming that reconstruction involves a copy that is deleted at some pre-PF level. In the derivational minimalist theory a copy is created by Move α, and deletion can take place both after and during SPELLOUT. In the radical minimalist theory there is no syntactic derivation, and thus there can be no deletion between the lexical input and LLF. The present approach will assume that copies of lexical categories can be present at (L)LF and that deletion of a copy can take place only in the interpretive components, as one effect of the SPELLOUT rule, in PF and presumably also in the post-(L)LF semantic interpretation.

In section 5.2, the minimalist theory of reconstruction involving post-SPELLOUT syntactic deletion is examined critically. I argue that certain data involving interaction between binding-theory principles and interaction between these principles and scopal reconstruction cannot be handled by this theory without internal contradiction. Furthermore I show that certain idiom interpretation facts that might appear to favor the LF copy-and-deletion theory over the PDFI approach in fact provide no such evidence. In 5.3 I turn to the PDFI approach and argue that it correctly accounts for the reconstruction data. When supplemented with the Projection Principle defended in chapter 1, the PDFI hypothesis also explains the asymmetrical behavior of adjuncts and arguments under reconstruction.

5.2 The Copy-and-Deletion Theory

Let us first summarize the standard minimalist theory of reconstruction (Chomsky 1993), beginning by considering (1):

(1) John wondered which pictures of himself Bill liked

Here the antecedent of *himself* can be either the matrix subject *John* or the embedded subject *Bill*. Movement consists of copying and subsequent deletion. The sentence in (1) is derived by movement of the wh-phrase *which pictures of himself* that leaves a copy behind. At LF the wh-phrase separates into the quantifier *which x* and its associate *x pictures of himself*. FI requires one of the two copies of both the quantifier and the associate to delete. The copy of the wh-quantifier in spec-CP must remain, presumably for interpretive reasons or perhaps also to satisfy the Wh-Criterion. The associate, however, may delete in either position. If the higher copy remains, the anaphor will take the matrix subject *John* as its antecedent; if the lower copy survives, then the antecedent of the anaphor will be the lower embedded subject *Bill*.

A fuller account of reconstruction has to be more complex, however. Complements and adjuncts behave differently under reconstruction: in (2a) but not in (2b) the pronoun *he* can take *John* as its antecedent. This appears to correlate with the fact that the NP *John* is in a complement in (2b) and in an adjunct in (2a):

(2) a. Which claim [that John made] was he willing to discuss
    b. Which claim [that John was asleep] was he willing to discuss

The data in (2) raise two problems within a minimalist approach where all relevant conditions hold at LF. First, it must be ensured that (the copy that contains) the complement "that John was asleep" in (2b) is not deleted at LF in the reconstructed position, so that principle C applying here can exclude the impossible association between *he* and *John*. This situation contrasts with that in (1), where the complement of the noun optionally "reconstructs",—that is, either copy may be deleted by LF. Second, the different behavior of adjuncts and complements must be accounted for: if the principle C violation in (2b) is due to the complement's presence in the reconstructed position, then the adjunct in (2a) must have the option of not similarly occurring there. Thus the greater freedom of adjuncts also needs an explanation.

To ensure that (2b) is excluded, Chomsky suggests that reconstruction must apply if possible, and provides reasons why reconstruction is not legitimate when *himself* takes *John* as its antecedent in (1). His suggestion is that at LF the anaphor has to cliticize to the verb of which its antecedent is an argument. Thus the LF representation of (1), on the reading where the NP *John* is the antecedent of the anaphor, will be in the relevant respect like (3a):

(3) a. John self-wondered which pictures of t Bill liked
    b. John self-wondered which x Bill liked [x pictures of t]

Reconstruction of the associate *x pictures of t* then results in a representation like (3b), but here the chain [self,t] is reasonably taken to violate some locality constraint (it would "break the chain (*self, t_{self})" (Chomsky 1993, 41). So reconstruction cannot and therefore does not apply when the anaphor takes the matrix subject as its antecedent in (1) as in (3). Nothing prevents reconstruction from applying in (2b), however, and therefore by Chomsky's preference principle reconstruction must apply, causing principle C to prevent coreference.

To account for the difference between (2a) and (2b), Chomsky adapts an idea of Lebeaux's (1989) to the minimalist framework. Lebeaux proposed a theory in which principle C applied at all points in the derivation and adjuncts could be attached at any stage in the process. Principle C thus applied both before and after the Wh-movement in (2b), accounting for the lack of coreference here. In (2a), principle C similarly applied at both stages, but the adjunct was attached only after movement had taken place, hence coreference was allowed: at the pre-movement stage the adjunct, containing the R-expression *John* that would be c-commanded there by the coreferential pronoun, is not yet present in the structure.

In Chomsky's approach the solution is essentially the same. The insertion of adjuncts, but not of complements, is unordered with respect to the application of Move α. Since copies are left by movement rules, a copy of the complement but not of the adjunct will necessarily be created in the Move α launching position. Thus a copy of the complement but not of the adjunct must remain present in the reconstructed position in cases like (2) by the preference principle, leading to non-coreference by principle C only for the complement internal R-expression. (The fact that a moved complement must be inserted before Move α is a consequence of Chomsky's extension requirement on the generalized transformation GT he proposes. Insertion of a subtree into another must always extend the target tree. Insertion of adjuncts is an exception to this requirement.)

There are a number of problems with the approach outlined. Immediately noticeable are two stipulations that need improvement. Neither the preference principle for reconstruction nor the assumption that adjuncts behave exceptionally with respect to the extension requirement seems explanatory. In Lebeaux's theory the fact that adjunct but not complement insertion was unordered with Move α followed from the Projection Principle: this entailed that complements must but adjuncts need not be present at D-structure. But this rationale is not available in the standard minimalist theory, where D-structure and the Projection Principle are rejected.

Barrs (1986) discusses several potential problems with an approach to reconstruction where the quantifier and its associate separate at LF. For example, he points out that it is not clear why a post-LF algorithm that recovers restricted quantification from LF representations where the quantifier and its restriction are separated should be preferable to a system where the whole phrase is reconstructed at LF and scope is determined beyond LF.

An additional problem is created by examples like (4a) where the anaphor is in the associate of a wh-in-situ.

(4) a. *John wondered when Mary saw which pictures of himself
    b. John wondered [which pictures of himself] when Mary saw t

If the arguments in chapter 2 are correct, then the overt and the LF Wh-movement of the standard Principles and Parameters framework are both constrained by Subjacency and thus exhibit the same cluster of properties in general. In order to capture this generalization, they must therefore be expressed by the same mechanism. In a derivational theory this means that wh-in-situ must involve LF movement. If so, the anaphor in the associate of the wh-in-situ should behave in the same way as the anaphor in the associate of the moved wh-phrase, since at LF the two do not differ in any relevant respect. We therefore expect that at least one possible LF representation of (4a) will be (4b). If binding principles apply at LF, this results in the incorrect prediction that the anaphor here can take the higher subject *John* as its antecedent. There is no immediately obvious nonstipulative reason why pied piping of the associate should be possible with overt but not with covert Wh-movement.

This problem does not arise in the radical minimalist theory, where the cluster of properties standardly associated with Move α is captured by chains. The LF structure of (4a) will be (5) with the contentive element, the wh-phrase, remaining in situ for morphological reasons (as discussed in chapter 4).

(5) *John wondered SM_x when Mary saw [which pictures of himself]$_x$

A different set of problems arises from the preference principle that reconstruction must apply if possible. As noted above, this has a somewhat dubious status to start with. We probably should not try to explain or motivate it, however. The example in (6) indicates that the solution involving this principle is likely to be incorrect. (Barrs 1986 uses an example with the same structure to argue a related point.)

(6) Mary wondered [which claim that pictures of herself disturbed Bill] he made
    (Compare: 'Mary wondered [which claim that pictures of herself disturbed him] Bill made')

In (6), the anaphor forces the associate *x claim that pictures of himself disturbed Bill* to occupy the nonreconstructed position, hence no preference principle can cause reconstruction to enable the proper application of principle C. Indeed, no matter which position the associate occupies, a problem arises. If it is in the higher position then principle C cannot apply correctly; if it is in the lower, reconstructed position, then the anaphor-antecedent relation becomes illegitimate.

Scope-reconstruction phenomena provide further evidence against the preference principle. Consider (7):

(7) Mary wondered how many pictures of herself did everyone paint

This can have the "distributive" reading characteristic of scopal reconstruction: "Mary wondered about everyone what the number of pictures of herself that that person painted was." If the structure is analyzed as involving reconstruction of the quantified wh-phrase, as argued by Cinque (1991), Rizzi (1990) and Frampton (forthcoming), among others, then the requirement of principle A appears to lead to a contradiction. Reconstruction must take place on the distributed reading, but the anaphor *herself* associated with the matrix subject requires that no reconstruction take place. The two requirements could be simultaneously satisfied only if the outer shell of the NP were in the reconstructed position:

(8) Mary wondered x pictures of herself everyone painted how many x

A structure like (8) seems implausible, however, both syntactically and semantically. The reconstructed element would be a nonconstituent and the structure would contain an unbound variable.

The examples in (6) and (7) show that the standard account is problematic in those cases where different principles pose different requirements on the position of the contentive category. Note that Lebeaux's theory has no difficulty in accounting for these cases. He explicitly argues that while principle C holds at *all* stages in the derivation, principle A must be satisfied only at *some* point. Hence in (6) coreference is excluded at the pre-movement level, whereas principle A is satisfied after movement has taken place. Similarly, Lebeaux assumes that scope relations may be determined at any point in the derivation. So the "scope-reconstructed" reading in (7) is due to the pre-movement configuration, while principle A is again satisfied after movement. Similarly (mutatis mutandis) for the other cases.

The evidence thus suggests that within a minimalist framework it is not sufficient to assume that *either* the antecedent or the trace position involved in a movement/chain-type relation contains a copy of the lexical material. At the level where the interpretive constraints (including the binding theory) apply, *both* positions need to contain a copy. This assumption is in effect a more faithful adaptation of Lebeaux's theory to the minimalist framework.

Chomsky (1993) gives an argument that appears to create problems for this multiple-copy hypothesis. He points out that in an example like (9) the idiomatic interpretation of *take a picture* (i.e., photograph) is available only on the reconstructed reading, that is, when the antecedent of the anaphor is not *John* but *Bill*:

(9) John wondered which pictures of himself Bill took t

This follows from his LF-deletion theory under the natural assumption that the idiomatic interpretation here is possible only if the idiom *take ... picture* forms a contiguous unit at LF. If only one copy can be present at LF, then idiom interpretation requires the copy to be in the reconstructed position, preventing anaphoric connection between the anaphor *himself* and the matrix subject *John*.

The hypothesis that copies are present in both positions of the relevant chain appears to be incompatible with this explanation: the requirement for idiomatic interpretation can be satisfied by the lower copy and principle A by the higher one. No strong argument can be based on this, however, since we can assume that anaphoric connection between *John* and *himself* is prevented by the understood subject of the noun *pictures*, which on the idiomatic interpretation must be coreferential with the subject of the matrix verb. (See Williams (1985) for a relevant discussion of thematic control.) Chomsky in fact notes that an intervening understood subject can block coreference with the matrix subject in a case like (10) (where the intervening subject is clearly structurally represented as the trace of *Mary* in the thematic AP-spec position):

(10) *John wondered how angry with himself Mary was t

The same account (modulo the difference between structurally represented versus thematically present empty subjects) carries over to (9). Note the background assumption, though: two chain-internal copies of the same element cannot have different referential relations. There is no "sloppy identity" in chains. Thus the understood subject, intervening between the anaphor and its antecedent, is associated with the subject of the embedded clause in both copies. (See the next section for more on the nondistinctness requirement relevant here.)

Other cases parallel to (9) that Chomsky presents as evidence for his theory are also handled by the same analysis. Consider his examples, (11)–(14):

(11) a.   John wondered what stories about us we had heard
      b.   *John wondered what stories about us we had told
      c.   John wondered what stories about us we expected Mary to tell

(12) a.   John wondered what opinions about himself Mary had heard
      b.   *John wondered what opinions about himself Mary had

(13) a   They wondered what opinions about each other Mary had heard
      b.   *They wondered what opinions about each other Mary had

(14) a.   John wondered how many pictures of us we expected Mary to take
      b.   *John wondered how many pictures of us we expected to take (idiomatic sense)

Chomsky comments on these examples in a footnote: "Cases [in (11)] correspond to the familiar pairs *John (told, heard) stories about him*, with antecedence only possible in the case of *heard*, presumably reflecting the fact that one tells one's own stories but can hear the stories told by others; something similar holds of the cases in [(12) and (13)]" (Chomsky 1993, 49n.50).

Thus an account of (11) must involve the assumption that an understood subject of the NP *stories about us* is in some sense present at least in (11b), controlled by the subject of the verb *told*. But given this assumption, the position of the wh-phrase *what stories about us* is irrelevant: principle B, applying within this phrase, will exclude (11b) but not (11a,c), wherever the wh-phrase is located. There is no evidence in (11) for the claim that the category is only in one position at LF.

As for (12) and (13), in a parallel to the analysis of (9) Chomsky presumably assumes that the ungrammaticality of the (b) examples is due to reconstruction having to take place. The anaphor, then, is separated from its putative antecedent by the embedded subject *Mary*. But as Chomsky observes in the quoted footnote, the considerations having to do with understood subjects extend also to these examples. Thus in "Mary had opinions about X" the NP "opinions about X" must have an understood thematic subject controlled by the NP *Mary*. Hence principle A will be violated, independently of the question of the LF position of this category. Finally, the situation in (14) is the same as in (11). (14b) is ungrammatical for the same reason as (11b): given the NP-internal understood subject, principle B is violated wherever the wh-phrase is located.

Additional evidence for the assumption that at LF a category is present in both its reconstructed and its surface position is provided, as a reviewer reminds me, by examples involving topicalization like (15) and (16), noted by Barrs (1986):

(15) a. *Him_x $John_x$ likes
      b. Him_x $John_x$ said Mary liked
      c. $Himself_x$ $John_x$ likes

Assuming that these should differ from their nontopicalized counterparts at LF, it is not clear how they can be treated in terms of reconstruction. The hypothesis that there is a copy in both the "reconstructed" and the topicalized positions of the chain of the topicalized category immediately resolves this problem. The account carries over to other cases, for example clefting in (16), on the assumption that these involve head-raising (cf. Brody 1993).

(16) a. It's him that John likes

b. It's him that John said Mary liked

c. It's himself that John likes

(Barrs considers and rejects an approach similar to the multiple-copy hypothesis. His main reason is the "PRO-movement" structure (17):

(17) John tried PRO to get arrested e

Given a copy approach, there will apparently be a copy of PRO present in the object position in (17). This, however, is illegitimate; it will be excluded by whatever restricts the distribution of PRO, incorrectly excluding the structure. The problem will not arise, however, if PRO is defined not in terms of its feature composition but in terms of its position in chains: say as a particular type of empty chain-head (cf. Brody 1985)).

In sum, while reconstruction phenomena appear to necessitate a copy in the "reconstructed" position, there is evidence that the lexical category is equally present in the "surface" position. One possible conclusion is that the minimalist approach is wrong and the constraints in question should hold at one or more pre-LF levels. However, the principles in question (scope and binding) have to do directly with interpretation and thus should clearly hold at the semantic interface. The assumption that LLF is this interface can be maintained if both (all) copies must be present here. Reconstruction, then, must not involve deletion in the syntax. This means that no derivational mechanism is necessary to treat the phenomenon.

5.3   Partially Determined Full Interpretation

Within the radically minimalist theory, there can be no reconstruction in the standard sense, since this involves the application of Move α. A copy-and-deletion theory like Chomsky's is also excluded in principle, since no syntactic deletion is possible in a syntax in which there is no derivation between the lexicon and LF apart from lexical insertion. However, the reconstruction data show clearly that a category can function as if it were present in a position in its chain that does not correspond trivially to its PF position. Suppose, then, that a copy of the category, present in this position at LLF, will be deleted as part of the effect of the SPELLOUT rule mapping between LLF and PF. Notice that this does not resurrect Move α within the syntax in a different guise. I assume simply that chains contain copies of the contentive category instead of empty category traces. A category is then represented by a chain, in which each member that is c-commanded by the contentive element is a copy of the contentive category. There is no deletion in syntax at all, hence no Move α, although there is a deletion rule during SPELLOUT, at PF. (Alternatively, we can take Form Chain to create layered traces, dispensing with PF deletion of lexical material.)

A further requirement on copies will be necessary. To see why, consider for example a chain headed by an NP. Suppose that a different N-complement is inserted in the two copies of the NP—say "the claim that he left" shares a chain with its "copy": "the claim that she is nice" (ignoring, for the sake of simplifying the example, the difference between NP and DP). Clearly this must not be allowed. Presumably such a situation is excluded because a chain cannot contain conflicting lexical specifications.

Notice that the possibility of creating a copy of the NP in which no element is inserted in the N-complement position is excluded by the contextual requirements projected from the lexicon. Thus the principle prohibiting conflicting lexical specifications in a chain will generally ensure that where a copy of an XP has been created, lexical insertion will insert only copies of the same elements in each copy of the XP. The lexical contextual requirements of X will be satisfied by the same elements in each copy of the XP, and the same holds recursively for Y and YP contained in XP.

Such an analysis, which assumes that a chain may contain multiple copies of its contentive element, is compatible with the principle of FI, since we take the units that are the input to FI to be chains as before. FI does not restrict the internal construction of the elements that the rules of interpretation take as their input. The proposal in effect makes the interpretively relevant position of the contentive category indeterminate within its chain: the contentive category can occur in more than one chain position at LLF. Since certain aspects of the interpretation are dependent precisely on the chain-internal position of the contentive category, it follows that the interpretation of the structure will be indeterminate in these respects. Hence the name of the approach: Partially Determined Full Interpretation (PDFI). (Notice that the principle according to which a chain can contain at most a single contentive/scope marker, suggested in earlier chapters, must now ignore copies and refer to independent contentives/ scope markers.)

According to the PDFI hypothesis there is only one deletion rule in the grammar: an effect of the SPELLOUT rule. There is no deletion within syntax proper, since there are no derivations at all (apart perhaps from projection and lexical insertion). Principles of interpretation will carry out deletion of the extra copies present at LF. Thus there is no simplicity argument here; I do not argue that the deletion rule can be eliminated. The argument is directly empirical and aims to show that the appropriate location for these deletion rules is outside syntax.

Reconsider first the apparent contradiction in (6):

(6) Mary wondered [which claim that pictures of herself disturbed Bill] he made

Recall that here the reconstruction requirements of principle C and of the anaphor are different. The proper application of principle C requires reconstruction, but the anaphor *herself* inside the associate has a legitimate antecedent only if no reconstruction takes place. Under PDFI, the LF structure of (6) will be like (18):

(18) Mary wondered [which claim that pictures of herself disturbed Bill] he made [which claim that pictures of herself disturbed Bill]

Principles A and C of the binding theory can now apply to this representation without contradiction. Principle C excludes an R-expression that is coreferential with a category that c-commands it (in any of the positions where it is present)—hence coreference between *he* and *Bill* is correctly excluded. Principle A requires a local antecedent for the anaphor in at least one of its positions and therefore the matrix subject can be a legitimate antecedent of the anaphor.

Take next the adjunct-complement asymmetry:

(19) a. Which claim [that John made] was he willing to discuss
     b. Which claim [that John was asleep] was he willing to discuss

In (2), reproduced here as (19), the complement has to have a copy in both positions to ensure that principle C prevents coreference of the complement-internal R-expression with the embedded pronominal subject. The adjunct, however, need not be present in both positions. On the coreferential reading it must not be present in the lower one to avoid exclusion by principle C. Thus the relevant structures are as in (20):

(20) a. [Which claim that John made] was he willing to discuss [which claim]
     b. [Which claim that John was asleep] was he willing to discuss [which claim that John was asleep]

The fact that an adjunct does not need to adjoin to both copies follows from the assumption that syntactic structures are projected from the lexicon. The complement must be present in both copies, since otherwise the selectional requirement of the head noun in at least one of the two copies would not be satisfied. Furthermore, the same complement must be present in both copies of the NP to avoid a clash of lexical specifications. The adjunct, however, is free not to appear in the lower copy: there is no general requirement of strict identity on these copies. As long as the two copies do not contain different adjuncts there is no feature clash.

Notice that the principle C violation in (20b) cannot be voided by assigning a different reference to the NP *John* in the two copies: this again leads to a clash of specifications. It is not possible to leave the lower copy of this NP without a reference, either. If this NP had no reference it would not qualify as an argument and therefore it would not be able to satisfy the projectional requirement of its predicate *was asleep*.

This type of adjunct-argument asymmetry shows up not only in connection with elements that are proper subparts of the category on which the chain is built but also where this concerns the chain-forming category itself. Thus in (21) the adjunct *near John* forms a chain and creates no principle C violation, in contrast with the chain of the selected PP *to John*.

(21) a.   Near John$_x$, he$_x$ saw a snake
     b.   *To John$_x$, he$_x$ gave an umbrella

(22) a.   Near John$_x$, he$_x$ saw a snake $\emptyset_x$
     b.   *To John$_x$, he$_x$ gave an umbrella to John$_x$

The explanation of this contrast is similar to the account given of (20), with the difference that here apparently it is necessary to invoke a null category trace for the adjunct. In (21a) the presence of a copy of the adjunct is not forced by selectional requirements, hence no copy is needed. There is, then, a legitimate structure where no copy is present and thus principle C is not violated. The grammaticality of (21a) shows that positions c-commanded by the contentive in the chain do not necessarily contain a copy of the contentive. The presence of a copy is generally forced only by selectional requirements. Null categories cannot satisfy these. Where no such requirement makes a copy appear, the position can contain a null category chain member, as in (22a).

In (21b), in contrast, because the verb *give* selects the preposition *to*, this element or its copy must be in place. The selectional requirements of *to* (or those of the verb via the preposition *to*) in turn force the presence of an argument NP, that must have properties, including referential ones, nondistinct from those of the NP *John* included in the head of the chain. Hence the LLF structure must be along the lines of (22b), resulting in a principle C violation. (Postal's 1993 discussion of WCO contains examples in which he judges reconstructed object bound names to be grammatical although he accepts that these are "hardly very natural." I have been assuming throughout that principle C excludes also names bound from object positions; see chapter 3 above. I assume that the same is true for reconstructed names. I have no interesting theory to explain why the effects are weaker than in the subject-bound cases. As for WCO, see Brody 1994 for an approach in terms of the PDFI theory that can resolve some of the problems that Postal raises.)

Consider the scopal reconstruction problem in (7), reproduced here, and its LLF structure in (23).

(7)   Mary wondered how many pictures of herself did everyone paint

(23) Mary wondered [how many pictures of herself] did everyone paint [how many pictures of herself]

The scope of the quantifer *how many* is ambiguous in both examples, both the "reconstructed" and the "nonreconstructed" readings are available since there is a copy of this quantifier both in and outside the scope of *everyone*. Principle A allows coreference of the anaphor with both the matrix and the embedded subject since a copy of the anaphor is present in both the higher and the lower position, and principle A, just like the scopal-interpretation configuration, has to be satisfied only in some position of the chain.

Turning to NP-chains, the assumption that these involve copies is problematic. (24a), for example, would have the (L)LF representation (24b), incorrectly excluded by principle C (cf. Lebeaux 1989, Chomsky 1993):

(24) a. The claim that John was asleep seemed to him t to be beside the point
      b. The claim that John was asleep seemed to him the claim that John was asleep to be beside the point.

Chomsky suggests that "[o]ne possibility is" that the root position of the A-chain "enters into the idiom interpretation (and, generally, into Θ-marking), while the head of the chain functions in the usual way with regard to scope and other matters" (Chomsky 1993, 42). As for root positions, we can be more general: as discussed in chapter 1, root positions of (A- or A'-) chains are involved in lexical projectional requirements, including theta marking. As for scope assignment in A-chains, this may involve positions other than the head of the chain—take the quantifier-lowering phenomenon: "Some senator is likely to speak at every rally" (May 1977; Chomsky 1981). Arguments exist that non-head positions of A-chains are relevant for principle A of the binding theory (cf. Belletti and Rizzi 1988; Barrs 1986).

An obvious solution could be the following. Suppose the category in the Case-marked position was deemed to satisfy the selectional requirements holding in the root position of the A-chain. Then a copy in the root position is optional, as in all other positions of the A-chain. If either a copy or a null category may occur in all non-head positions of the A-chain, then the principle C violation in cases like (24a) can be avoided.

But this approach appears not to work. It predicts that in (25a) coreference between *he* and *John* will be impossible on the scope-reconstructed reading, where a copy of the QP must appear in the root position of the chain. Similarly, in (25b) overlap in reference between *John* and *them* should be incompatible with the presence of the anaphor that again forces the presence of a lower copy. No such incompatibility can be observed:

(25) a. Some friend of John seemed to him to have spoken to every senator

   b. The claim that pictures of themselves disturbed John seemed to them to have been an overstatement

It seems, then, that principle C, but not principle A or scopal reconstruction, ignores categories included in the root position of A-chains. One could make sense of this on the assumption that A-chain roots and categories contained in them are invisible only to principles of obviation. Modifying the standard thematic visibility condition (Chomsky 1981) slightly, suppose that categories that are dominated (immediately or not) by a Caseless position are not visible arguments for theta-role assignment because they cannot refer. Assume further that the ability to refer is not a necessary condition for linking (in Higginbotham's (1983, 1985) sense) to an antecedent. This can provide the desired distinction: referential obviation principles cannot apply to A-chain roots, but scopal reconstruction and anaphoric-linking-type reconstruction can take place also in A-chains.

Finally, let us note a consequence of the approach for head chains. If these also involve copies, then yet another often cited argument for a derivational theory collapses. It has been argued that the head-movement constraint (or whatever it follows from) is better stated on derivations than on output representations, on the basis of structures where a head H/1 moves to another H/2 that in turn moves further (cf. Chomsky 1987; Chomsky and Lasnik 1993). This can be exemplified by V to AgrO to T to AgrS movement under the split-inflection approach or by movement of the V + Infl complex to a higher verb, as in causatives, for example:

(26) a. J'ai fait partir Pierre
     b. CAUSE $[_x V_y I]$ t_x t_y
     c. CAUSE $[_x V_y I]$ $t_{x,y}$ t_y
     d. CAUSE $[_x V_y I]$ $[_x V_y I]$ V_y

The representation in (26b) appears to violate the HMC, even though each step in the derivation obeys it. As I noted in chapter 1, the argument is valid only if it is desirable and feasible for a trace to have only a single index, a moot point in any case. If a trace can have more than one index, then the (LF-)representation of (26a) can be well-formed, as in (26c). But it now follows from the general copying approach that the relevant indices will be in place in the (L)LF representation of (26a), namely (26d). The latter will not violate the HMC, and thus this argument for a derivational theory also falls away. (For a discussion of Chomsky's recent (1994) comments on such an approach, cf. appendix 1 to chapter 1.)

5.4 Conclusion

I argued in this chapter that reconstruction need not and must not involve syntactic deletion, and that therefore an adequate account can be given of this phenomenon in a restrictive, nonderivational framework. I showed that no valid evidence exists from the interaction of idiom interpretation with the binding theory for the claim that at (L)LF the copy of the contentive in the overt position must in some cases be deleted.

By assuming that LLF chain construction involves copies of the contentive element instead of empty categories c-commanded by the contentive, a preference principle for reconstruction was rendered unnecessary. The Projection Principle, together with a nondistinctness requirement on chain-internal copies, made the reconstruction data explainable in the radically minimalist framework. The adjunct-complement reconstruction asymmetry also followed from the Projection Principle.

References

Aoun, J. and Y. A. Li (1989). "Scope and Constituency." *Linguistic Inquiry* 20, 141–172.

Aoun, J. and Y. A. Li (1993). "Wh-Elements In Situ: Syntax or LF?" *Linguistic Inquiry* 24, 199–238.

Baltin, M. (1987). "Do Antecedent Contained Deletions Exist?" *Linguistic Inquiry* 18, 579–595.

Barrs, A. (1986). *Chains and Anaphoric Dependencies.* Ph.D. diss., MIT, Cambridge.

Belletti, A. (1988). "The Case of Unaccusatives." *Linguistic Inquiry* 19, 1–34.

Belletti, A. and L. Rizzi (1988). "Psych-Verbs and Theta Theory." *Natural Language and Linguistic Theory* 6, 291–352.

Borer, H. (1986). "I-Subjects." *Linguistic Inquiry* 17, 375–416.

Borer, H. and Y. Grodzinsky (1986). "Syntactic Cliticization and Lexical Cliticization: The Case of Hebrew Dative Clitics." In H. Borer and Y. Grodzinsky, eds., *Syntax and Semantics 19: The Grammar of Pronominal Clitics.* Academic Press, New York.

Boskovic, Z. (1993). "D-structure, Theta Criterion and Movement into Theta Positions." Ms., University of Connecticut and Haskins Laboratories.

Brody, M. (1985). "On the Complementary Distribution of Empty Categories." *Linguistic Inquiry* 16, 505–546.

Brody, M. (1987). "On *Chomsky's* 'Knowledge of language.'" *Mind and Language* 2, 165–177.

Brody, M. (1990a). "Case Theory and Argumenthood." Paper presented at the annual GLOW meeting, Cambridge, England.

Brody, M. (1990b). "Some Remarks on the Focus Field in Hungarian." In *UCL Working Papers in Linguistics 2.* Department of Phonetics and Linguistics, University College London, London.

Brody, M. (1991a). "Economy, Earliness and LF-based Syntax." In *UCL Working Papers in Linguistics 3.* Department of Phonetics and Linguistics, University College London, London.

Brody, M. (1991b). "Notes on an LF-based Grammar." Ms., Institute of Linguistics, Hungarian Academy of Sciences, Budapest.

Brody, M. (1992). "A note on the Organization of the Grammar." In *UCL Working Papers in Linguistics 3*. Department of Phonetics and Linguistics, University College London, London.

Brody, M. (1993). "Theta Theory and Arguments." *Linguistic Inquiry* 24, 1–23.

Brody, M. (1994). "Phrase Structure and Dependence." Ms., University College London, London.

Browning, M. A. (1987). "Null Operator Constructions." Ph.D. diss., MIT, Cambridge.

Burzio, L. (1986). *Italian syntax*. Reidel, Dordrecht.

Cheng, L. (1991). "On the Typology of *wh*-Questions." Doctoral Dissertation, MIT, Cambridge.

Choe, J. W. (1987). "LF Movement and Pied Piping." *Linguistic Inquiry* 18, 348–353

Chomsky, N. (1981). *Lectures on Government and Binding*. Foris, Dordrecht.

Chomsky, N. (1982). *Some Concepts and Consequences of the Theory of Government and Binding*. MIT Press, Cambridge, Mass.

Chomsky, N. (1986a). *Knowledge of Language: Its Nature, Origin and Use*. Praeger, New York.

Chomsky, N. (1986b). *Barriers*. MIT Press, Cambridge, Mass.

Chomsky, N. (1987). "Comments on Reviews by Alexander George and Michael Brody." *Mind and Language* 2, 178–197.

Chomsky, N. (1991). "Some Notes on Economy of Derivation and Representation." In R. Freidin, ed., *Principles and Parameters in Comparative Grammar*. MIT Press, Cambridge, Mass.

Chomsky, N. (1993). "A Minimalist Program for Linguistic Theory." In K. Hale and S. J. Keyser eds., *The View from Building 20: Essays in Linguistics in Honor of Sylvain Bromberger*. MIT Press, Cambridge, Mass.

Chomsky, N. (1994). "Bare Phrase Structure." Ms., MIT, Cambridge.

Chomsky, N. and H. Lasnik (1993). "Principles and Parameters Theory. In J. Jacobs, A. von Stechow, W. Sternefeld and T. Vennemann, eds., *Syntax, an International Handbook of Contemporary Research*. W. de Gruyter, Berlin.

Cinque, G. (1991). *Types of A'-Dependencies*. MIT Press, Cambridge, Mass.

Clark, R. (1983). "Parasitic Gaps and Split Anaphora." Ms., University of California, Los Angeles.

Contreras, H. (1984). "A Note on Parasitic Gaps." *Linguistic Inquiry* 15, 704–713.

E-Kiss, K. (1984). "The Order and Scope of Operators in the Hungarian Sentence." *Groninger Arbeiten zur Germanistischen Linguistik* 24, 82–126.

E-Kiss, K. (1985). "Parasitic Chains." *The Linguistic Review* 5, 41–74.

Engdahl, E. (1983). "Parasitic Gaps." *Linguistics and Philosophy* 6, 5–34.

Engdahl, E. (1984). "Parasitic Gaps, Resumptive Pronouns and Subject Extractions." Ms., University of Wisconsin, Madison.

Epstein, S. D. (1991). "Derivational Constraints on A'-Chain Formation." *Linguistic Inquiry* 23, 235–259.

Fiengo, R. and R. May (1990). "Anaphora and ellipsis." Ms., City University of New York and University of California, Irvine.

Fiengo, R. and R. May (1994). *Indices and Identity.* MIT Press, Cambridge, Mass.

Fiengo, R., J. Huang, H. Lasnik and T. Reinhart (1988). "The Syntax of *Wh*-in-Situ." In *Proceedings of the West Coast Conference on Formal Linguistics,* vol. 7, Stanford Linguistics Association, Stanford University, Stanford.

Frampton, J. (1990). "Parasitic Gaps and the Theory of *Wh*-Chains." *Linguistic Inquiry* 21, 49–77.

Frampton, J. (Forthcoming). "The Fine Structure of *Wh*-Movement and the Proper Formulation of the ECP." In W. Chao and G. Horrocks, eds., *Levels of Representation.* Foris, Dordrecht.

Freidin, R. (1978). "Cyclicity and the Theory of Grammar." *Linguistic Inquiry* 9, 519–549.

Haegeman, L. (Forthcoming). *The Syntax of Negation.* Cambridge University Press, Cambridge, England.

Haegeman, L. and R. Zanuttini (1991). "Negative Heads and the NEG-Criterion." *The Linguistic Review* 8, 233–252.

Higginbotham, J. (1983). "Logical Form, Binding and Nominals." *Linguistic Inquiry* 14, 395–420.

Higginbotham, J. (1985). "On Semantics." *Linguistic Inquiry* 16, 547–593.

Higginbotham, J. and R. May (1981). "Questions, Quantifiers and Crossing." *The Linguistic Review* 1, 41–80.

Hoekstra, T. (1988). "Parasitic Gaps: A Unified or Composed Chain?" Ms., Rijksuniversiteit Leiden, Leiden.

Hornstein, N. (1994). "An Argument for Minimalism: The Case of Antecedent-Contained Deletion." *Linguistic Inquiry* 25, 455–480.

Hornstein, N. and A. Weinberg (1990). "The Necessity of LF." *The Linguistic Review* 7, 129–167.

Horvath, J. (1992). "Anti-c-Command and Case-Compatibility in the Licensing of Parasitic Chains." *The Linguistic Review* 9, 183–218.

Huang, J. (1982). "Logical Relations in Chinese and the Theory of Grammar." Ph.D. diss., MIT, Cambridge.

Hudson, R. (1984). "Multiple (Alias 'Parasitic') Gaps." Ms., University College London, London.

Jaeggli, O. (1980). "Remarks on *to*-Contraction." *Linguistic Inquiry* 11, 239–245.

Johnson, K. (1991). "Object positions." *Natural Language and Linguistic Theory* 9, 577–636.

Kayne, R. (1981). "Two Notes on the NIC." In A. Belletti, L. Brandi and L. Rizzi eds., *Theory of Markedness in Generative Grammar*. Scuola Normale Superiore, Pisa.

Kayne, R. (1983). "Connectedness." *Linguistic Inquiry* 14, 223–249.

Kearney, K. (1983). "Governing Categories." Ms., University of Connecticut, Storrs.

Kitagawa, Y. (1987). "Subjects in Japanese and English." Ph.D. diss., University of Massachusetts, Amherst.

Koizumi, M. (1993). "Object Agreement Phrases and the Split VP Hypothesis." In: *MIT Working Papers in Linguistics* 19.

Koopman, H. and D. Sportiche (1991). "The Position of Subjects." *Lingua* 85, 211–258.

van de Koot, H. (1994). "On the Status of the Projection Principle in the Minimalist Program." In *UCL Working Papers in Linguistics 6*. Department of Phonetics and Linguistics, University College London, London.

Koster, J. (1978). *Locality Principles in Syntax*. Foris, Dordrecht.

Koster, J. (1987). *Domains and Dynasties, the Radical Autonomy of Syntax*. Foris, Dordrecht.

Laka, I. (1993). "Unergatives That Assign Ergative, Unaccusatives That Assign Accusative. In: *MIT Working Papers in Linguistics* 18, 149–172.

Lappin, S. (1992). "The Syntactic Basis of Ellipsis Resolution." In S. Berman and A. Hestvik, eds., *Proceedings of the Stuttgart Ellipsis Workshop*. Arbeitspapiere des Sonderforschungsbereichs 340, Bericht 29. IBM Germany, Heidelberg.

Lappin, S. (Forthcoming). "The Interpretation of Ellipsis." In S. Lappin, ed., *Handbook of Contemporary Semantic Theory*. Basil Blackwell, Oxford.

Larson, R. (1988). "On the Double Object Construction." *Linguistic Inquiry* 19, 335–391.

Larson, R. and R. May (1990). "Antecedent Containment or Vacuous Movement: A Reply to Baltin." *Linguistic Inquiry* 21, 103–122.

Lasnik, H. (1985). "Illicit NP-Movement: Locality Conditions on Chains?" *Linguistic Inquiry* 16, 481–490.

Lasnik, H. (1989). *Essays on Anaphora*. Reidel, Dordrecht.

Lasnik, H. (1992). "Case and Expletives: Notes Toward a Parametric Account." *Linguistic Inquiry* 23, 381–407.

Lasnik, H. (1993). "Lectures on Minimalist Syntax." Ms., University of Connecticut, Storrs.

Lasnik, H. and M. Saito (1984). "On the Nature of Proper Government." *Linguistic Inquiry* 15, 235–289.

Lasnik, H. and M. Saito (1992). *Move α*. MIT Press, Cambridge, Mass.

Lasnik, H. and T. Stowell (1991). "Weakest Crossover." *Linguistic Inquiry* 22, 687–720.

Lebeaux, D. (1989). "Relative Clauses, Licensing and the Nature of the Derivation." Ms., University of Maryland.

Lightfoot, D. (1979). *Principles of Diachronic Syntax*. Cambridge University Press, Cambridge, England.

Longobardi, G. (1991). "In Defense of the Correspondence Hypothesis: Island Effects and Parasitic Constructions in Logical Form. In C.-T. J. Huang and R. May, eds., *Logical Structure and Linguistic Structure*. Kluwer, Dordrecht.

Longobardi, G. (1992). "Proper Names and the Theory of N-Movement in Syntax and LF." Ms., University of Venice.

Manzini, M. R. (1983). "Restructuring and Reanalysis." Ph.D. diss., MIT, Cambridge.

Manzini, M. R. (1992a). *Locality*. MIT Press, Cambridge, Mass.

Manzini, M. R. (1992b). "Categories in the Parameters Perspective: Null Subjects and V-to-I." In W. Abraham and E. Reuland, eds., *Language and Knowledge*. Kluwer, Dordrecht.

Manzini, M. R. (1993). "Locality Theory and Parasitic Gaps." Ms., University College, London.

May, R. (1977). "The Grammar of Quantification." Ph.D. diss., MIT, Cambridge.

May, R. (1979). "Must COMP-to-COMP Movement be Stipulated?" *Linguistic Inquiry* 10, 719–725.

May, R. (1985). *Logical Form*. MIT Press, Cambridge, Mass.

May, R. (1988). "Ambiguities of Quantification and *Wh*: A Reply to Williams." *Linguistic Inquiry* 19, 118–134.

McDaniel, D. (1989). "Partial and Multiple Wh-Movement." *Natural Language and Linguistic Theory* 7, 565–604.

Nakajima, H. (1986). "Kiss's Case-Transmittance Approach and the Binding Path Approach to Parasitic Gaps." *The Linguistic Review* 5, 223–245.

Nakajima, H. (1990). "Another Response to Kiss." *The Linguistic Review* 7, 365–374.

Nishigauchi, T. (1990). *Quantification in the Theory of Grammar*. Kluwer, Dordrecht.

Pesetsky, D. (1982). "Paths and Categories." Ph.D. diss., MIT, Cambridge.

Pesetsky, D. (1987). "WH-in-Situ: Movement and Unselective Binding. In E. Reuland and A. ter Meulen, eds., *The Representation of (In)definiteness*. MIT Press, Cambridge, Mass.

Pesetsky, D. (1989). "Language Particular Processes and the Earliness Principle." Ms., MIT, Cambridge.

Pesetsky, D. (1992). "Zero Syntax." Ms., MIT, Cambridge.

Pollock, J.-Y. (1989). "Verb Movement, Universal Grammar and the Structure of IP." *Linguistic Inquiry* 20, 365–424.

Pollock, J.-Y. (1993). "Notes on Clause Structure." Ms., University of Picardie, Amiens.

Postal, P. (1971). *Crossover Phenomena*. Holt, Rinehart and Winston, New York.

Postal, P. (1993). "Remarks on Weak Crossover Effects." *Linguistic Inquiry* 24, 539–556.

Reinhart, T. (1991). "Non-Quantificational LF." In A Kasher ed., *The Chomskian Turn*. Basil Blackwell, Oxford.

van Riemsdijk, H. (1983). "Correspondence Effects and the Empty Category Principle." In Y. Otsu et al., eds., *Studies in Generative Grammar and Language Acquisition*. International Christian University, Tokyo.

van Riemsdijk, H. (1987). "Movement and Regeneration." Ms., Tilburg University.

Rizzi, L. (1982). *Issues in Italian Syntax*. Foris, Dordrecht.

Rizzi, L. (1986a). "On Chain Formation." In H. Borer and Y. Grodzinsky, eds., *Syntax and Semantics 19: The Grammar of Pronominal Clitics*. Academic Press, New York.

Rizzi, L. (1986b). "Null Objects in Italian and the Theory of *pro*." *Linguistic Inquiry* 17, 501–557.

Rizzi, L. (1990). *Relativized Minimality*. MIT Press, Cambridge, Mass.

Rizzi, L. (1991). "Residual Verb Second and the *Wh*-Criterion." Ms., University of Geneva.

Saito, M. (1989). "Subjects, Specifiers and X'-theory." In M. Baltin and A. Kroch, eds., *Alternative Conceptions of Phrase Structure*. The University of Chicago Press, Chicago.

Sportiche, D. (1983). "Structural Invariance and Symmetry in Syntax." Ph.D. diss., MIT, Cambridge.

Starke, M. (1994). "On the Format for Small Clauses." Ms., University of Geneva.

Stowell, T. and F. Beghelli (1994). "The direction of Quantifier Movement." GLOW abstract, Vienna.

Taraldsen, K. T. (1981). "The Theoretical Interpretation of a Class of Marked Extractions. In A. Belletti, L. Brandi, and L. Rizzi, eds., *Theory of Markedness in Generative Grammar, Proceedings of the 1979 GLOW Conference*. Scuola Normale Superiore, Pisa.

Tonoiko, S. (1991). "Operator Movement in Japanese." Ms., Meiji Gakuin University and MIT, Cambridge.

Watanabe, A. (1991). "*Wh*-in-Situ, Subjacency and Chain Formation." Ms., MIT, Cambridge.

Wilder, C. and D. Cavar (1993). "Word Order Variation, Verb-Movement and Economy Principles." Ms., Max-Planck-Gesellschaft, Berlin and University of Potsdam, Potsdam.

Williams, E. (1984). "*There*-Insertion." *Linguistic Inquiry* 15, 131–153.

Williams, E. (1985). "PRO and Subject of NP." *Natural Language and Linguistic Theory* 3, 297–315.

Williams, E. (1986). "A Reassignment of the Functions of LF." *Linguistic Inquiry* 17, 265–299.

Wyngaerd, G. and J.-W. Zwart (1991). "Reconstruction and Vehicle Change." In F. Drijkoningen and A. van Kemenade, eds., *Linguistics in the Netherlands*. John Benjamins, Amsterdam.

Index